SPORTING ADVENTURE

By the Same Author

KING GEORGE V AS A SPORTSMAN
THE MODERN FOWLER
A FALCON ON ST PAUL'S
THE LIFE OF SIR HENRY SEGRAVE
SPEED—THE LIFE OF SIR MALCOLM
    CAMPBELL
KAYE DON—THE MAN
      ETC. ETC.

"From the farthest wastes of Spitzbergen."

SPORTING ADVENTURE

By

J. WENTWORTH DAY

Editor of "The Illustrated Sporting and
Dramatic News"

WITH THIRTEEN PHOTOGRAVURE PLATES AND
FIFTY LINE DRAWINGS BY
"FISH-HAWK"

LONDON
GEORGE G. HARRAP & CO. LTD.
SYDNEY   BOMBAY   TORONTO

First published September 1937
by GEORGE G. HARRAP & CO. LTD.
182 *High Holborn, London, W.C.*1

Reprinted October 1937

Made in Great Britain. Printed at the St Ann's Press,
Timperley, Cheshire

TO
NERINA

I knew the Spring was come, I knew it even
    Better than all by this, that through my chase
In bush and stone and hill and sea and heaven
    I seemed to see and follow still your face.
Your face my quarry was, for it I rode,
My horse a thing of wings, myself a God.

                St Valentine's Day
              WILFRED SCAWEN BLUNT

FOREWORD

THREE years ago Lord Beaverbrook said to me, in one of those moments of electric inspiration which disturb the philosophic pool of his mind: " Jimmy, you're fool enough to lie on your stomach in a marsh watching birds. Well, write about them before you die of cramp. Birds have more adventure than most people. They see more of the world than any of us. So write about them. Humanize the urbanized."

So I proceeded to write about them. The result, in part, is this book. It is the record of scattered, stolen days from a life which began in the country, is wedded to the country, and will, I pray God, end in the country. Most of us to-day, who must work for our living in the competition and chaos of cities, find a green peace of contentment and an enrichment of mind and health in the sports of the field or in the gentler delights of the flight of a bird, the blossoming of a tree, the scent of hedgerows in bloom, the sight and smell of the wet and lonely miles of the sea, the immense peace of moors and hills.

The more intense our speeded-up civilization, the more grossly material the mechanization of our thought and transport, the greater the human need for those old and simple things of the open air which began with the beginning of time. Standardization of thought and interest is the product of a board-school-ridden, film-produced civilization.

7

It is as deadening to the average city dweller, as fatal to the production of individuality, as the mob-psychologies of any of the 'isms' of political thought which threaten us with the final armageddon, the cataclysmic suicide of civilization.

The only retreat for the average man is a return to green fields, to natural pursuits, to the simple sports of rod and gun, to battlings with wind and tide, the elemental demands of horsemanship and marksmanship, the plain principles of country life. Through them comes that contented philosophy which Thoreau knew and Jefferies interpreted.

This book is merely the record of a countryman's occasional escapes from London. It is the record of days and week-ends snatched from one of the most competitive professions of to-day to rediscover the things which make life better worth living.

I have seldom or never, within the last seven years, taken more than a few days from my everyday work. But it has been possible in those few days to step back a century, to put from fifty to three hundred miles between London and my goal.

The result has been a re-invigoration of thought and enthusiasm, a quickening of health and, I hope, the retention of enough sense of humour to refuse to take present-day civilization at its own over-serious valuation. It has been a recurring adventure—an adventure possible to anyone.

One need not be very rich thus to escape. A little initiative, the reading of a map, the determination to get there—

the equal determination to drop the mantle of the town like a forgotten garment, for a few, particularly precious hours or days.

The increasing interest in nature study, the growing desire for country life, even if only at week-ends, the latent villager in the heart of almost every town-dweller, the robust love of an Englishman for a horse, a gun, or a ship—these are the future guarantees of the sanity and tolerant-mindedness of our race.

To those who have the old surge in their blood, the hunger for the smell of the sea, the love of a horse, the ache for wet woods and June dog-roses—to them this book will, I hope, bring some few hours of recaptured sights and scents and sounds, some imperfect echo of the simple joys and principles which have made the sense and strength of our race.

J. WENTWORTH DAY

WICKEN, CAMBS.,
July 17

The author desires to record his grateful thanks to the Editors of the " Evening Standard," " Daily Telegraph," " National Review," " Daily Express," " Country Life," " The Farmer's Weekly," and the Proprietors of the " Illustrated Sporting and Dramatic News," for permission to include all, or part, of articles which have appeared from time to time in their columns.

His thanks are due also to the Proprietors of " Country Life " for permission to reprint the extracts from Miss Dorothy Hartley's work " Thomas Tusser," to Mr Patrick Chalmers for the many quotations from his enchanting verses, to Mr E. D. Cuming for permission to quote a verse from his " Idlings in Arcadia," and to the author's representatives and the publishers, Messrs Macmillan & Co., for the quotations from the poems of that remarkable and scholarly Sussex squire, the late Wilfred Scawen Blunt of Crabbet Park, Crawley, the father of the present Baroness Wentworth.

CONTENTS

11

SPORTING ADVENTURE

CONTENTS

FULL-PAGE PLATES

We hear the year pass, as you heard it. Hear the crackling of the breaking frost, the silence of the winter snow, the lash of rain and the lapping of the floods. We know of the change of the wind in the night, and the song of the birds in the dawning, the bleating of lambs and the lowing of cattle. Then the spring days come, when the plough is out continually. The level fields dry beneath the wind (the colours fading out in waves, as the clouds pass over, pulling up into the sky). The high tides wash against the marsh wall, the dykes are full, and the wild-fowl nest in the rushes. The year presses on so swiftly to full summer, and there blows the scent of the hay, and we feel the fear of rain. Without pause, it is harvest-time, and all East Anglia is yellow with corn and the sky is blue, and the slope of your land to the south is sunburnt ripe corn and the harvest-folk have been, and gone home again, and the barns are full, and Autumn is come . . .

Then, one night, it turns cold; and we lie closer for warmth and stay waking a little, thinking of the things we must do—speedily, for it is the winter.

DOROTHY HARTLEY

JANUARY

I

Behold his punt now ride the restless wave,
A little speck, scarce scanned from off the shore.

Hear his proud thunder floating on the tide!
Mark the dread fiat of the death-winged shower!

T. HUGHES

UNDER a half-moon veiled in cloud, a long, low, silver-grey shape, pointed fore and aft, manned by two men, the muzzle of a nine-foot gun peeping over its fore-deck, slips down the creek on the first whisper of a rising tide. Mud-flats glide by like dull silver. Curlew whistle; peewits weep on the landward marshes; a whicker of pinions cuts the sky above; redshank, those restless spirits of the shore, pipe and flute up the lonely miles of the estuary. The night's silence is alive with the clang and call of feeding fowl.

For eight long miles, between us and the blank spaces of the North Sea, there lies the broad, moon-silvered bosom of an estuary that knew the Dane, that knows no modern town

upon its banks to-day. The tide gurgles in the crab-holes. A little wind runs through the sea lavender on the saltings. A heron, silver-grey, stands ankle-deep in the sliding tide. We pass him within a dozen yards before he sees the low, sinister shape of the gun punt, and, suddenly, hoarsely, flaps over the flats, the night sky ringing with his fear.

Somewhere out on the muds that, inch by inch, are going under as the tide flows, there are widgeon feeding——hundreds of them. The whistle of the cock birds, the purring growl of the hens, come in a babel. And beyond, on some lonely spit, as yet unseen in the moon haze, are geese——geese in battalions, fresh from Novaya Zemlya or Spitsbergen, geese that have seen no man save Lapp or Finn.

The moon strikes a path of softened silver down the seaway ahead of our bows. With your breast resting upon an inclined plank, your left arm over the four-inch freeboard, your left hand working a short, submerged paddle, the punt creeps almost imperceptibly forward. In front, on a level with the eye, lies in its cradle the nine-foot long barrel of a gun, an inch and a half in bore, a hundred pounds in weight, loaded with a pound of shot, breeched for recoil with a rope strong enough to hold a horse.

Behind, cramped into a space six feet long and three feet wide, lies the second punting partner, his right hand and arm working a paddle over the side. Thus, with only the eye-level of two heads visible above the deck of the punt, the craft glides down to the sea and the salt-flats where the geese feed under the moon.

20

"The broad moon-silvered bosom of an estuary."

An hour of such back-breaking work and the clamour of the great, grey birds, fresh from the Arctic, grows to a gabbling tumult.

Faintly they can be seen, a dense huddled mass, feeding on the long green *zos* grass on a mud-flat which is lessening every minute in area as the tide flows.

A hundred yards, ninety, eighty . . . heads go up, a sentinel cranes his neck, there is an indefinable wave of alarm. . . . *If only we can gain that extra deadly ten yards.* . . . The punt glides forward . . . the gunner's right hand tips the butt of the great gun, his right foot kicks the bottom boards . . . a sudden hoarse clamour of alarm, a windy threnody of pinions. The whole mud-flat seems to lift in a wave of surging feathers . . . BOOM . . . a tongue of flame sears the darkness, an enormous plume of smoke belches over the water, the report rolls and re-echoes like the crash of a field gun . . . and the punt shoots back yards in the water under the recoil.

Geese drop like sacks of wheat, sending up fountains of water. The sky is alive with the skirl and clamour of fowl, the whistle of pinions. The water is dotted with dead geese, furrowed by wounded striving to escape. The shoulder-guns settle them.

When all are gathered there is a count. Sixteen. As good as one will get this winter.

That is one of the luckier nights in this fascinating sport of punt-gunning, which is now in progress on the lonely creeks. There are not many of us who practise this most arduous form of sport. It is a cold, wet, ill-rewarded business. Deer-stalking is child's play by comparison. Grouse-shooting is a drawing-room affair. Pheasants and partridges are quarry for sybarites.

Thus, secure in the priggish knowledge of our own barbarian exclusiveness, we big gunners have a special affection for the bitter months which are our own season.

Punt-gunning is not the butchery which ill-informed and facile critics imagine it to be. Let them try a night afloat under stars which wink with frost, when the punt sides whiten, when the snow falls harshly, when the tide strains arms, shoulders, and muscles, when one's wetted sleeves and sodden jacket freeze stiff. Let them try hour on hour of patient stalking . . . to see the result ruined at the last moment by a watchful sentinel, an unsuspected heron, a shrieking redshank, or by an unwise movement on the part of the punter himself. I have been out seven week-ends running, seen thousands of fowl, and never fired a shot. That is the normal side of the picture.

Yet it is the most fascinating sport in these islands, costing little in equipment and free to all below high-water mark.

One remembers days on all the lonely creeks and bays from the wide waters of Chichester Harbour, where Bosham nestles at the head of its idyllic creek to Pagham, lonely, overlooked by the tower of old Sidlesham Church, to Rye Bay, where the black duck gather in worthless thousands, and so round the coast to the siren-haunted seaways of the Thames estuary and the Swale, where the duck gather in hundreds undreamed of on the south coast.

I shall not soon forget that cold morning eight years ago when our punt glided out of the mists of dawn and showed us the sudden rare vision of a great white spoon-bill, a bird extinct in England for a century, feeding not fifty yards off our bows. That was on the Blyth Sand, off Southend. That spoon-bill was left to feed and preen himself.

The Crouch, nineteen miles of tidal river, the Roach, the Blackwater—that mighty river of gunners where thirty punters once killed 704 geese at a joint discharge, only sixty years ago—the Colne, with its oysters; the Stour, broad as a small sea; the Deben, where FitzGerald sailed his little boat and wrote of Omar; the Alde, sluggish between its miles of cattle marshes, the river which inspired Crabbe . . . here are rivers for the man with courage and an adventurous heart. You can buy a second-hand punt and gun for £25 or so.

And if you want real risks in treacherous seaways where the fowl are in thousands go to the Wash, where the sea fog

shuts down like a blanket and the seals sleep far out on the sands like giant slugs.

There are rivers, creeks, and bays in plenty for the punter, risk of death by drowning and exposure, small chances of big bags . . . and when the big shot comes, be it ten birds or half a hundred, you forget the cold, the bitter dawns and thunderous eves, the wet and the wind. It is the last of the old, primitive sports of the gun, this big gunning on the fringes of the sea for the fowl that are wild as the Arctic wastes which bred them.

But it is not all such a desperate business of frost, snow, and bitter cold. There are the quieter days of early autumn when the duck are new in from the Baltic.

There comes to mind such an early dawn, out from Mersea Island, a year ago.

Four o'clock in the morning and as black as a nigger at the bottom of a well. A thin chill wind from off the sea stirs the willows which stand straight and stark in the shaft of yellow light from the window.

Outside, the darkness is abysmal. The cows in the orchard at the back of my fowling cottage snuffle in the blackness. Below the orchard the footpath wavers down a field to the saltings and the slow tides that suck and eddy through all the miles of Essex creek and estuary which surrounds this island of the Dane.

Presently we are out, sea-boots crunching through the dew-soaked grass, electric torch flashing on the huddled backs of sleeping cattle. A hundred yards down the field we climb the sea-wall—that frontier between the desert and the sown. Here the fields end and the salt-marshes begin.

Somewhere in the blackness down on the mud where the oyster pits end and you sink up to your ankles at each step we stumble on the duck punt. Long, low, and grey, shaped like a slender cigar, with sides no more than eight inches high she lies there in the beam of the torch, a slender silvery-grey craft, twenty-two feet six in length, with a three-feet-six beam, tapering to narrow pointed bow and stern.

She is decked fore and aft—a boat built to lie flat and almost invisible on the sea, to draw no more than three inches of water, to creep stealthily like a sliding shadow over the shallows and into the little rills which run up into the miles of mud-flats.

Down the mud to the tide edge we launch her, a shadow in the utter blackness of the hour before dawn. It is silent still, uncanny.

Curlew whistle distantly. A great black-backed gull barks hoarsely out on a sand-bar. The light wind drums in the rigging of unseen fishing-boats. We have two miles to go before dawn.

Yachts loom up white and ghostly as we slip down the tide. Luckily there are not so many of them in the fairway as there were a month ago. Autumn is here. The first chill winds are blowing—so the butterfly yachtsmen, cap-proud in their white tops, have gone back to London in the horrid shiny motor-cars that made this once delectable isle a veritable Blackpool beach in summer. They and their strident Cockney owners are gone—only a few of the real old shell-back type, the real salt-water men like Sydney Gowing and Rennie Reeves, Jimmy Jones and 'Bungie' Dixon remain, one with the fishermen and the winklers, the fowlers, and the flight-shooters, "the brethren of the coast."

Then it is that the wildfowler, most of all the punt-gunner, that deer-stalker of the tidal flats, comes into his own. For with the frosts and the north winds come duck and geese in sibilant thousands, fowl from Lapland and Finland, from wooded lakes at Scandinavia and the bleak flats of Pommern and the Lithuanian marshes.

CURLEW

The first of them are here already. That is why we are afloat with the big gun, its first outing this season. For to stalk wildfowl on open salt water, in full view of scores, possibly hundreds, of watchful eyes, calls for a vessel as nearly invisible as possible, and a gun that will kill at twice the range of an ordinary gamegun.

27

Hence the weight and might of our artillery, the fantastic design of the punt itself. It is an attenuated shallow little death-trap, no vessel in which to encounter squalls or the short seas that are born of a storm.

So, since the equinoctials have a horrid habit of bursting in upon you suddenly in a welter of wind and rain, we breathe a shade more freely when the punt's bows swing into the broad waters of a shallow creek that goes creeping three miles up through the marshes.

It is half a mile wide, but the tide is down, only just beginning to flow, and the main channel winds and twists through incredible mountain-ranges of mud, past miniature valleys and diminutive mountains, a curious abnormal world of its own, a microcosm of a mountainous sea coast.

But here the mountains are of mud. If they are six feet high they loom almost to the majesty of six hundred feet. The valleys are only a yard or two in width, yet any valley come upon suddenly as the punt noses silently round the bend in the channel may yield its sudden quacking uprush of ducks surprised at their food or sleep.

Dawn shows now—a faint grey glimmer along the sea to our rear. A band of silver spreads and runs for a few minutes along the farther horizon of the sea. Then the light floods up the sky.

Smacks in the distance take on finite shape. Beyond them, two miles out in the estuary, laid-up cargo boats loom on the water like fantastic floating castles, unreal, immense.

It is light enough now to shoot. Overhead gulls flit

jerkily, ghosts on the pale breath of dawn. Curlew squabble and away off on the flats a heron flaps heavily, his hoarse *fraa-a-ank* filling the silence. Redshank whistle noisily, and far off, a dog barks at a marsh farm: peewits wail.

A mile and a half now since we left our own home 'hard' and not a sign of a duck. Almost it seems as though we are too soon in the season. The punt's bows nose gently round a promontory, only a foot high, but immense as we lie, chest-down, on the floorboards of this little creeping vessel, our faces not four inches above sea-level.

What is that ahead? Seven, eight, nine, ten—a dozen or more dark hunched forms sleep on the tide edge. And beyond them five or six others, much larger. And beyond them others scattered in twos and threes along the edge of the water.

PEEWIT

29

Teal and a bunch of mallard with outlying teal beyond. They are at least a hundred and twenty yards off and some, at any rate, are awake, feeding, their suspicions quick to kindle should we make the least sound, should a boot scrape on a floorboard or a hand-paddle be dropped with a splash.

My companion nudges my elbow. It is the signal. I take the lanyard attached to the trigger of the big gun in my right hand, tip the barrel slightly with my left, sight down it, head well drawn back. *Crash!* My companion's boot rattles on the floorboards—and in an instant the ducks are up, quick as light.

The lanyard is jerked, a tongue of flame sears the grey half-light—the report thunders and rolls, crashes and re-echoes from bank to bank, a muttering boom that thuds across the marshes to be heard two miles away. The punt quivers to the recoil, surges backward, and as the smoke blows away we see five, six, seven teal and a mallard down in the water. Two are cripples, soon polished off with a shoulder-gun, the rest dead.

It is the first shot of the season, a lucky one. There will be many grey dawns and wet nights, white days of frost and bitter nights of snow when we shall come home empty-handed from miles of salt-water creepings. But this is still butterfly weather, this first shot an easy baptism.

II

In days when courtesy is dim,
  And speech grown less polite and plainer,
You never fail to find in him
  The deference of the old retainer;
He speaks about the crops and birds,
  About the weather and the stubbles,
With some apologetic words
  Of stiffness and rheumatic troubles.

ALFRED COCHRANE
" The Old Gamekeeper," in *Later Verses*

Moonlight sifting through naked branches. Gaunt firs stark against a Valkyriean night sky; moving clouds and a thin wind keening in the tree-tops, running like mice through the dead and rusty bracken—and under the shoulder of the hill, White, the keeper, Nip, the terrier, and myself. Nip, silky, tiny, a bare two feet over all, scarce ten pounds in weight, was the spearpoint of the expedition—a winter night's badger dig.

That night was fifteen years ago, yet it lingers with all the fearful joy of illicit memories. It was in one of those old, wide deer-parks for which democracy now has no use— a place where the oaks that knew Edward Tudor stand memorial for dead centuries, the beech glades are still spirit of the old forest lands, and the bracken slopes harbour the tall deer.

To-day such parks are targets for taxation. But on that

night fifteen years ago owls hooted in the oaks, ducks spattered on the lake and, somewhere on the hillside, a grey old boar badger grunted morosely in the subterranean fastnesses of a gigantic sett whose ramifications tunnelled the hill for yards. Hounds had kennelled him up late that afternoon.

It was his second escape from being 'chopped' in a fortnight.

So we decided to dig him out, put him in a bag and move him to the opposite side of the county, where an enlightened landowner desired badgers on his property.

It took us four hours and a half, two spades, a mattock, a beetle and wedges, two pairs of prodigious badger-tongs, and three hours of heroism on the part of Nip, who pinned the badger for three hours until the mattock and the spade, the wedges and the tongs got down to him through root and rock and earth and drew him forth. So when I read that Mr

So-and-so dug a badger yesterday weighing thirty-six pounds, or that Lord So-and-so's hounds chopped a badger instead of a fox late on Wednesday, my mind goes back to all the immemorial days when we have dug badgers.

Now this digging out of the badger is no ignoble thing. At its best it is a work of philanthropy whose object is to remove unwanted badgers from over-populated regions and transport them to estates where they are wanted. At its eighteenth-century worst it was sheer butchery.

Few kill the badger wantonly. For the badger does a great deal of good. He eats mice, young rats, wasps' nests, beetles, worms, slugs, and a host of other unpleasant and unnecessary creatures. But he does not eat game. Pheasants and partridges are safe.

The fact is that he is, in his habits and habitat, extremely ursine. Indeed, he has been described frequently and picturesquely, but quite erroneously, as " the last of the British bears."

Observe a badger in the moonlight—slouching, pointed nose to ground, his great hams hunched, his stiff coat glistening in the wan light, his grunt breaking the slow silence of night in an ancient wood, his mien that of one who fears nothing on earth save man and his dogs—and there, if you like, is the bear in little. And what more bear-like than this nightly plucking of berries, this scraping out of wasps' nests, this eager licking-up of the combs of wild honey, this thick-hided imperviousness to pain and the stings and arrows of infuriated wasps?

c

No animal in Britain has a thicker hide than the badger. No animal burrows quicker or burrows farther. His underground dwelling, known as a sett, mastered the principles of municipal flat-planning untold thousands of years before the Karl Marx tenement arose in Vienna.

For the badger digs out a system of rooms and passages far more complete than the average small modern flat. He has one room to sleep in and one to eat in, a lavatory at the end of a cul-de-sac, even occasionally a well for water, small holes at the end of passages in which dead mice, beetles, and roots are stored, and an abhorrence of dirt.

The badger brings his bedding, pounds and pounds of hay and straw, out to air in the early sun on most sunny mornings before the average human is awake. I have seen ten square feet of badger bedding spread out on the lawn under the windows of an old house three hours before the maids were up, with the old grey pair grunting and sniffing round it. Sometimes a fox shares the sett, but badgers do not like foxes as a rule. The fox smells. But more than once a rabbit and her family have been discovered living side by side with a badger *ménage*.

Badger digging is first and foremost the exercise of unparalleled cheek and heroism on the part of a minute terrier, coupled with the exercise of a great deal of digging and bad language on the part of one, two, or more human beings. The terrier goes into the sett, rouses the badger, drives him into one of the cul-de-sacs and there holds him, by the simple process of biting occasionally at his backside, until rescue in the form of spades and badger tongs at length arrive.

Badger tongs are just like sugar tongs, with the difference that they are 223 times larger and heavier. You grip the badger with them by the scruff of his neck and haul him out. If you do not grip him properly he will grip you—and the badger can bite clean through a man's foot.

Occasionally, of course, the badger-digger himself takes the risk. For example, I remember Sir Alfred Pease telling me how only six years ago at a badger dig on a Yorkshire hill they located him thirty feet down a tunnel big enough for a man to crawl into. So Sir Alfred crawled the thirty feet into the hill, along a narrow earthen tunnel in pitch blackness, his eyes and nose full of falling dust, pushing the badger tongs in front of him. Behind him crawled another man. And behind him yet a third. And behind him yet once again a fourth. And the heels of the fourth stuck out just beyond the mouth of the sett.

When at last, in that nightmare blackness, Sir Alfred located the badger, grunting with fury, a bare yard in front of his unprotected face, he poked out with the badger tongs, groped blindly, caught hold of something and pulled. And the second man laid hold of Sir Alfred's heels and pulled, while the third man pulled the heels of the second, and the fourth the heels of the third. Out in the open air, far away in Yorkshire where the sun shone, three men and two boys sought valiantly to dislocate the waggling feet of the fourth.

35

Two old women and a horse looked on while six small terriers set up a Greek chorus on their own.

Thus, pulling, spitting out dirt, panting and sweating, out the human train was drawn, with, at the end of it, Sir Alfred hanging on grimly to a gigantic badger whom he had gripped by the forepaw only. A moment after the tunnel fell in with a crash. Which proves that not always do the terriers have all the fun. But then there are not so many Alfred Peases in this world.

III

JANUARY 17TH, 1823. Saw a vast quantity and variety of fowl on the Avon. A Hooper came and pitched within forty-five yards of me. I fired both barrels at him, but I might as well have spit at him. He appeared to be of a large size, and 'hooped' as he sat in the water, and bore a very beautiful and majestic appearance. He was afterwards shot at with ball near Christchurch. The man missed him and killed a cow.

The Shooting Journal of JAMES EDWARD,
SECOND EARL OF MALMESBURY

The birds have learned wisdom. Something of a revolution has come about among them. Half-guessed-at instincts, the inherited memories of their forefathers have come to light and life. There are many wiser birds in England now than there were a few weeks ago. They have all suddenly grown up. The snow was the cause of it.

If that hard winter, of which there have been many portents, should come, the mortality among birds will be lower than if it were to descend suddenly, unheralded, without warning—a white and paralysing foe, of which the birds would know nothing. Now they are better prepared.

Most birds, after all, live a very short life. Cats, small boys with air guns, brick-traps, and other engines of death, combine with a host of furred and feathered enemies to make their lives a continual see-saw between life and death.

That is why probably not one in ten of the present generation of birds had ever realized what snow and frost could really mean. When it came, they were puzzled; they were frightened. Nut-hatches hammered on tree trunks that had suddenly, inexplicably become hard as iron; blackbirds groped in ditch-bottoms and were frightened when their beaks rang on ice-bound earth where the day before had been soft soil. Mallard sat far out on the ice of the mere or paddled dejectedly around the shore, their brains groping with this strange phenomenon that had turned the waters of home into a sheet of glass.

It was all very disturbing. It happened in a few hours—almost as short a time as it would take any duck of well-regulated habits to fly out from the mere to the uplands, dine wisely and return to his ancestral waters. Suddenly the face of the land that they had known as a kindly face was changed to a mask of irony. A strange alchemy, unknown before in their lives, turned the old familiar places into forbidding haunts that denied them food, froze their flesh and nipped the very roots of their being. The healthy zest for food-hunting was prolonged beyond the bounds of its old enjoyment. It became a weary, monotonous task. Hunger came—a gripping, gnawing hunger such as they had not known before.

The pangs of that hunger awoke somewhere a buried instinct, the resurgence of a primeval sixth sense, a sense which taught them that these new strange conditions must be met by new methods. That was why the young blackbirds of the year went to the red haws in the hedges when the grub life of the ditch bottoms was no more. That was why the pipits left the moors and departed to the streamside meadows where still a surge and swell of dark waters hurried valleyward between white and crackling rims of ice, where still here and there a spring bubbled darkly amid the snow

DISH-WASHER, OR PIED WAGTAIL

and spread like a stain of blood on the dazzling face of the land. The pipits found there the food denied them on the moors. Not much it is true, but a little is better than nothing.

The wagtails, wiser in their generation—and the dish-washers are a very wise race, wiser than that flippant flip of the tail would have you believe—left the streamside and departed instead to the wold pastures and the cattle-yards where seas of heaving sheep kicked up the soil, or steaming cattle, moving slowly in the rotten straw, uncovered a wealth of horrible—but eatable—insect life.

It was different with the ducks. Either the mallard has

no brains, is too dull a fellow to think far ahead, or he possesses a sturdy heroism which prompts him to defy the frost. In any case, when the mere was frozen, he sat out in the middle with his wife. Fat, black, fluffed-out dumplings they looked. Meanwhile the widgeon and teal had gone seaward. Moorhens were in the hedgerows. The dabchicks, a brainless lot at best, for their brains are in their feet, moped about in little parties, looking like horrible old men who had met to launch a joint grouch against the Government. The change was quite beyond them, something too utterly revolutionary either to be met or accepted. They just stayed about because they had not the wit to do otherwise. But the mallard still hung on, calm in their fat and philosophy.

What would have happened had it continued for weeks? The haws would have given out, stockyards cannot feed all the pipits, and grain stacks have an end. Clearly there would have been more birds than food. Then we should have had the old melancholy tale. Silent, bitter nights, a white world under a white moon, trees black on the lee-side, and high up in the branches the dark hunched forms of roosting birds. Every now and then in the cruel silence of the snow, a lurch, a crackle of breaking twigs, a thump on the snow— and one more frozen corpse for the stoats in the morning.

There would have been dead moorhens in the hedges, partridges tracked to death in the snow, blackbirds lying stark and pitiful in the shrubbery; tits, very small and still, stiff under the dining-room window—all the pathetic toll of little lives which lots of people accept as inevitable when hard winters come. Lots of others, of course, stop to think. Somehow the sight of little bodies does not please them. Little bodies cannot be taken with equanimity. Such people feel that these little bodies would be much better alive.

They are the sort of people who stop to think three times in the day—morning, midday, and tea-time—when they put out crumbs and marrow bones, scrape up the odd sweepings of chicken food and the crusts that no one wants, and leave them on the lawn. These are the people who can tell you afterwards how they sat secretly by the window and watched moorhens and starlings, rooks and blue-tits, an old cock pheasant and even a ragged, impudent magpie all feeding together—a sight, after all, worth seeing.

Those are the people who, if a hard winter should come, will realize with the sportsman—although they themselves may not be sportsmen—that just as the wise man feeds his pheasants in winter, so the lover of small unconsidered birds, the little garden vagabonds, can give himself as great a pleasure by caring for those to whom wintry days are not a joy but just one bleak hour after another of hunger and hopeless search, to whom winter nights hold, each night more fully, the threat of death. It is worth thinking on.

IV

Hushed is the hairy Mammoth's roar
And gone the mastodon uncouth
Down to decay with dinosaur,
Aurochs, and fearsome sabre-tooth;
But you, small beast in hodden-gray,
Survive, and will, I take for granted,
Be here when I am dust, to play
In moonlit covers still unplanted.

PATRICK CHALMERS
Green Days and Blue Days

Every now and again somebody proposes to promote a Bill to prohibit entirely the use of the steel rabbit trap, either for rabbits or anything else. This raises a storm, and most of the sporting papers are up in arms about it. All sorts of ridiculous arguments are put forward that the measure, if made law, will kill the rabbit trade.

But personally, although I expect to kill at least two thousand rabbits each year on my own and other people's shoots, although I expect the rabbit to pay for at least half of my shooting rent, I should welcome this proposed Act.

The trapping of rabbits in steel gins is a brutal and barbarous business. Even the latest, so-called humane trap has very little to recommend it. For although it may not give the rabbit any great degree of actual physical pain, it may none the less mean that he is condemned to suffer for four or five hours in a state of acute fear, securely held by the leg until someone comes to break his neck.

42

Rabbits must be killed. But there are ways and different ways of doing it. You can shoot a rabbit, snare him, ferret him either to the gun, or into a purse net, long-net him, stalk him with a rook rifle, or knock him over with a stick.

But when it comes to the commercial killing of rabbits, which is an industry in such counties as Norfolk, Suffolk, Hampshire, Wiltshire, Dorset, Devon, Cornwall, and the Midlands, there is only one way to take the rabbit quickly and quietly and with the minimum of pain. That is to long-net him. I go long-netting rabbits every winter. Here is a night.

We set out from the keeper's house on a still and ghostly night, just as the clocks were striking ten, in a little village in that lost county of Huntingdonshire, which is still part of the very old soul of England. They have no manufacturing towns there, no factory chimneys, very few village omnibuses, and no reminder of the outward glittering world, except the brief occasional visits of that latter-day import, Mr Beverley Nichols. So you may say that Huntingdonshire, apart from the slugs on its garden paths, is comparatively unspoilt.

And in such remote parts of England, there and in Norfolk, where we stand, as it were, still rather like lost mariners, on the shores of that ancient invisible ocean of reeds and water, the old Fen, the old habits die hard. When we want a rabbit we net him.

I went out with my host, one of his keepers, a retired poacher, and a small long-legged animal who is by a terrier out of a collie. It is an odd but intelligent result.

43

There are eight keepers on that estate, " And," said my host, " we will see how many of them are awake. We will go and net some rabbits in the park, George, just as you used to! "

George grinned from mutton-chop to mutton-chop. This legalized audacity was too much for him. Thereafter we proceeded on illegal lines as though all the forces of keepers and the law were against us. Silently, under the shadowy edge of a covert, an old wood full of snoring owls and rabbit burrows that fell in like honeycombs beneath our feet as we walked, we set the net. It was five yards out from the wood's edge just inside the line of the dark shadow cast by a young moon.

In front lay the park, old and full of oaks. Once it was a home of deer. The great stags roared on its bracken slopes in the cold nights of November. There are no stags to-day. But there were ducks, spattering on the lake, coots clanking solemnly, the whistle of the wings of wildfowl overhead.

The net was out, a hundred yards of it, two feet high above the ground, with a drag and stretch of fifty yards in its lower half—it was run out and set on its sticks, pegged down and all ready in just over two minutes. That was because we were working with an old poacher.

And then the dog was sent out. Silently, like a creeping shadow, it slipped over the ground, a gliding ghost in the light mist, circling the park like a harrier. It rounded up those rabbits as a collie rounds up the sheep. There you will see the advantage of the collie cross. And because it was half a terrier, it had a nose for rabbits. But the collie cross stopped the other half from that sharp, sudden yelping which would have betrayed us.

In three minutes every rabbit within a quarter of a mile was on the move, rushing madly, headlong to the woods. We crouched by the net. Into it they came, swift, tumbling catapults of fur. They struck the net at headlong speed and rolled themselves up in it, inextricably. That is where the fifty yards of loose net in every hundred yards comes in.

It was all over very quickly. A quick pull and a stretch and the rabbit was dead. But there is rather more art in breaking a rabbit's neck when he is in the net than when he is out of it. That you must learn.

But in less than an hour and a half, we had set the net three times and taken forty-nine rabbits. That, we will say, was two sovereigns well earned, a certain relief to the tenant farmers' feelings, and a quantity of good, unspoiled food ready for the market. Now, this could not have been done so neatly, quietly, expeditiously, or painlessly by trapping. For one thing, not one of the seven other keepers heard us.

When I shoot in Devon or Cornwall I commonly kill pheasants with only one leg, partridges which hobble on stumps, rabbits that hop grotesquely on three legs. These are the victims of trapping. That is one side of the picture.

When I come back to London from East Anglia by the night mail from Thetford I travel frequently on a train that carries anything from 5000 to 35000 dead rabbits. Those Norfolk rabbit trains are an unknown part of English commerce. For rabbit-farming in Norfolk, and rabbit-killing, is a big business. Rabbits on the right land will produce a net profit of fifteen shillings an acre, as against two shillings and sixpence an acre from sheep on the same land.

These Norfolk rabbit trains are the other side of the picture. For most of the Norfolk rabbits are either shot or netted. They are far cleaner and tidier to look at—and better meat to eat than the trapped, miserable creatures of the West Country, whose blood and flesh just before the moment of death was soured and inflamed by terror. A rabbit that dies quickly and painlessly is far better eating than one which has been tortured in a trap.

A law prohibiting the use of steel traps will not stop us from shooting rabbits, which is a reasonable form of sport, and it will certainly not stop the rabbit. For the rabbit is inextinguishable. He is invincible. Neither civilization nor the cataclysms of Sodom and Gomorrah could destroy him. The rabbit, if need be, will outlast the race of man. He is a remarkable fellow.

FEBRUARY

I

Yet still . . . a northern charm shall fold you,
Though Shot shall shake the raindrops from his sides
　　Though you catch the drifting clamour
　　Through the sleet squall's sting and hammer,
Still the fight shall work its magic and the breathless
　　stalk shall hold you,
When the grey geese come calling off the tides!
　　　　　　　　　　　PATRICK CHALMERS
　　　　　　　　　　　Green Days and Blue Days

FOR many years no winter so severe had been known.
Morning after morning men had gone down to the river-
side to count the inches recorded on the white posts. Morning
after morning they told a tale of rising waters and hurrying
floods. Finally there came a dawn when a wan sun struggled
through the fog and gleamed across a waste of leaden waters.
Full three square miles in extent, they shone like a sea.

Mighty deeds had been done that night. In the grey quiet
hours betwixt moonrise and midnight a sudden hoarse
bellow, like the roar of a siege gun, followed by the thunder
of leaping waters, quivered through the night. Minutes of
anxiety and wonders passed. All knew what had happened;
none knew where matters would end. Then from the river-
wall a horse's hooves rang sharp and clear on the frosty air
and a horseman galloped madly out of the mist. At the Inn,
lonely amid its riverside willows, he halted, his horse's fore-
feet spurning the gravel. A hail and a halloo, and to the

crowd that tumbled out of the brightly lit Inn the story was told in a gasp: " She've blowed! Went off like a gun a mile furder up on Barway washes and blowed out a grut lump o' bank as big as a couple o' housen. The waters a'comin' thru' like waves o' the sea, and I've sin fower dead hosses in the river as 'tis. You'll niver stop her to-night—she'd carry a church away, let alone a boatload o' clunch. We've got the Bailiff out with a vengeance ternight and He'll mek it wuss 'fore marnin'! "

To the men who listened, rough, bearded, and uncouth, in mud-stained cords and battered hats, the River—be it Ouse or Nene or merely humble Cam—is the Eternal Feminine. ' She ' is their lover, their life, and their mortal fear. Life is lived with her; death comes sometimes from Her. Long nights on end they had tramped the river walls, their horn lanthorns and hurricane lamps glimmering weirdly through the blackness. Not a foot of all those miles of banks was left unsearched. Not a bend nor a dyke-head but was peered at and muttered over. For when ' She ' has ' riz ' it behoves all men to look well to the banks that spell safety of life and property. Before now a mere trickle through a rat's hole has next morning changed to a raging breach of forty feet in width.

The horseman's tale needed no elaboration. Its import was all too clear and serious.

Action followed—for these slow ' Fen tigers ' are speed itself when real necessity arises.

A boat was run out, men stumbled aboard, a line of heavy barges loaded gunwale deep with masses of tenacious gault (clay) were poled out into the sucking rush of mid-stream. The darkness swallowed them up. Within thirty minutes they had grounded a hundred yards north of a mighty breach in the great river wall of the swollen Cam.

The thunder of racing waters drummed through the night. In an hour, in a minute, months and years of work and watching had gone in a seething turmoil of shouting waters.

Where cattle had lowed there rang the hoarse challenge of white-crested waves. Through the great breach sixty feet across the flood poured in like billows of the sea. A lather of spume and spray wetted the faces of the watchers. A bitter nor'-easter whipped down the river and cut them to the bone. A flurry of snow, frozen hard as swan-shot, bit faces and ears alike. The line of boats groaned and creaked, plover wailed under the flying storm-wrack of the moon amid the clouds, and over all, the trampling floods flung a full-voiced challenge to the men who had dared curb and drain those one-time meres and mighty lakes. In a night their work had gone. The 'Bailiff of Marshland' had come into his own again, and for a week and a day his glittering miles would mock defiance at Man and all his works.

It was plain that the breach could not be 'plugged.' No boat, no three boats, could have been sunk in such a cauldron. They, like the section of bank that had been and now was *not*, would have been swept far out on the fens into battered nothingness.

So the boats lay still until the rush of waters should abate, and twenty men poled steadily back to the ancient Inn. There in a snug and sanded kitchen ale was mulled on the hearth and 'dogs-nose' brewed in pannikins.

With the dawn came realization. To north and south and far into the east a rippling sea winked back at the early sun. Bucking and struggling up-stream came a boat from Lynn whose red-nightcapped skipper told a tale of spreading waters. Other boats worked up river to the Inn. News flew backward and forward over the clink of pewter and the pungent clouds of 'niggerhead.' The rafters rang with the stamp of hobnailed highlows and the grunt and boom of many voices. All the types of Fenland were met together. There were men who had seen the broad Wash of Welney in flood from bank to bank and others who had sailed Vermuyden's Drain into the red eye of the setting sun.

Tales were told of drowned bullocks and reedstacks met floating down in mid-stream. Red-eyed and wizened, a little man spoke of a team of wild swans seen flying high over the Earith, while another boasted of the 'cartwheels' (crowns) that would be his for the skin of an old dog-otter shot that morning as he crouched on a semi-submerged dyke-bank.

But not every 'February fill dyke' or even a roaring March brings such disaster. Provided that the river banks hold, the broad 'washes,' often half a mile to a mile wide, which lie on either side the rivers of the Fens, will carry all the surplus water from the uplands of Huntingdonshire, Bedfordshire, Northampton, and the rest. For a few brief

"A tale of spreading waters."

weeks these broad grazing marshes, dry as a bone in summer, starred with cuckoo flowers, their dykes yellow with king-cups, become broad and noble rivers, echoes of the once-mighty meres of the old Fen.

The month of March 1937 saw the worst floods that we in the Fens had known for many years. Fifteen thousand acres of good fenland, the richest corn land in England, lay under water. Another 100,000 acres of land, worth from £20 to £70 an acre, was threatened by inundation. At the back of my house at Wicken in Cambridgeshire, three miles from the big break in Soham Lode, two hundred acres of my own land was from two to four feet under water.

That old house has seen five hundred years of Fenland mists and fogs, of flood and the threat of the sea tides. We who live in the Fens are a queer lot. Up in the 'Sheers' they call us 'Fen tigers' or 'Yellow bellies' and allege that we are web-footed, spotted on the stomach like toads, roisterous in our habits, murderous when roused, ambitious of power, rich and secretive.

There is reason for these conflicting attributes, these op-posing virtues.

We are Fen tigers because the whole life of the Fenman since the time of the Roman has been a struggle with the floods and a war against the Uplanders.

When Hadrian ruled in Britain and the Count of the Saxon shore sailed his galleys on the east coast, the Fens were a wild and desolate country, a place of meres; an ague-ridden race of amphibians snared fowl, netted fish, and walked

53

on stilts. They called us 'Cambridgeshire camels' in later years.

The Romans built the first catchwater drain in Lincolnshire. The Carr Dyke is their monument, even as the King's Delph preserves the memory of Canute, who ordered it to be dug westward from Whittlesey to Peterborough, after he had suffered an especially stormy voyage over the waters of Whittlesey Mere. The Tudors attempted drainage and failed.

The Carolean Kings bribed a Dutchman, Sir Cornelius Vermuyden, with a promise of 95,000 acres of land, to draw up the scheme of drainage which is the basis of our drainage system to-day. Vermuyden drew, planned, and drained. He succeeded. But not until the Fen tigers had risen against him, murdered his Dutch drainers, blown up his sluice gates, breached his great banks, stabbed his watchmen, thrown their bodies into the sullen, sluggish tides of Ouse and Nene, and reflooded tens of thousands of acres of the land which is to-day the richest of all England.

And then, when Vermuyden's work was done, and the Fens had become the granary of all England, we made war with the Dutch, and the Dutchman who had drained our Fens was obliged to sell his property. He died abroad, old, poor, and broken in health and riches.

To-day there are two million acres of the land in the Ouse Catchment Board area, with an annual rateable value of £3,000,000. That land is worth anything from £15 to £100 per acre. Nowhere in England is there land so rich. Just here and there, as in the Ormskirk district of Lancashire and round about Watchet in Somerset, there are areas almost equally rich but not one-hundredth part as vast. This 2,000,000-acre tract of upland and black, dyke-ruled flat fenland that runs on along into the melting horizon like the waves of an immobile sea, is drained by 560 miles of rivers, all feeding and comprising the great Ouse, which meets the tide at Denver Sluice and empties into the sea at King's Lynn.

It is an ironic reflection that whereas in the days of the Stuarts and afterwards we reclaimed most of these 2,000,000 acres of upland, swamp, and fen, we have, since 1914, in the vast knowledge of our vaunted modernism, allowed no less than 2,000,000 acres of arable land elsewhere in England to go out of cultivation.

And in that month of March 1937 it seemed as though our bungling bureaucracies of Government and the County Council-ridden plans of engineers had merely succeeded in putting back the clock three centuries. It was nothing less than a crime that 100,000 acres of fenland, in an age of electricity and vast engineering resources, should lie exposed to a peril of Nature which our forbears held in check by the crudest of methods.

Until sixty years ago there were vast, prairie-like expanses of corn lands on which no house was built. Every remote farm and stranded lonely village stood upon a hill or 'ey.' That was because of the imminent deadly peril of the flood.

In the old days they called the flood waters 'The Bailiff of Marshland' because when the bailiff was abroad people were put out of their houses without warning.

Then drainage improved, banks were strengthened, out-falls deepened, and confidence waxed. So they built farms and cottages of that hideous white Cambridge brick, the un-loveliest building material, in that bleak and bitter land. They built them where the sense of their grandfathers would never have allowed a house to be reared.

If the banks ever go there will be death and destruction over many a square mile. There will be women drowned in the night, babies floating among dead sheep and moaning cattle on the flotsam-strewn bosom of the waters. There will be men sitting on the roof-trees of lonely little houses that peer above the floods with a hard and startled air.

There will be no one to blame. It will just be " an act of God." It will merely mean that by an odd ironic stroke the Fens will have come into their own again.

The banks blew that March at Soham Lode and drowned the rich acres of Soham Mere, that one-time Saxon lake where Canute rowed in a barge to hear " the monks of Ely sing so merrily."

It was at Soham Mere one bitter winter that a fat Saxon, one Brithnoth, skated over the crackling, blue-black ice before the King to prove that it was fit and strong enough to bear the Royal weight on his way to Ely—the Isle of Eels and monks.

If the banks were to go at Denver and Littleport, the three centuries of work done by those great drainers, Sir Cornelius Vermuyden; my own ancestor, Sir Hugh Myddleton; Bishop Morton and the noble ' Company of Adventurers,' led by

Francis, Earl of Bedford, would be undone in a night, by one winter's snows and rains. All that flat and lonely land, desolate and rich, misty with the fogs, would go under.

There would be acres of shining water as there were in Saxon days, when Hereward the Wake, the last of the Saxons, held the Isle of Ely, a lone, forlorn citadel amid the bogs, against the conquering, mail-clad hordes of William of Normandy. To-day in a wet winter we sit in our Fenland houses and tremble. Three hundred years ago those rude and hairy forbears of ours, the Fen tigers, sang a quaint song, "The Powte's Complaint." It is a nice point whether the title accuses the versifier of being a poet, or whether it refers to the eel-pouts or burbots of the Fens, a hybrid—half eel, half fish—which, I imagine, we Fen people are commonly regarded as resembling:

Come brethren of the water and let us all assemble,
To treat upon this matter, which makes us quake and
    tremble;
For we shall rue, if it be true that Fens be undertaken
    (drained)
And where we feed in Fen and reed,
They'll feed both beef and bacon.

They'll sow both beans and oats where never man yet
    thought it;
Where man did row in boats ere undertakers bought
    it,
But, Ceres thou behold us now, let wild oats be their
    venture,
Oh, let the frogs and miry bogs destroy where they
    do enter.

> Behold the great Design, which they do now deter-
>   mine,
> Will make our bodies pine, a prey to crows and
>   vermine.
> For they do mean all Fens to drain, and waters over-
>   master;
> All will be dry, and we must die—'cause Essex calves
>   want pasture.

Thus, having called the Fenmen together against this dreadful design to drain their bogs, destroy their fevers,[1] enrich their lands, and ennoble their purses, the unknown poet of 1629 invokes the Fenman's god of that day, the Fenman's terror of to-day, and cries:

> Send us good old Captain Flood to lead us out to battel,
> Then tuppeny Jack, with scales on his back, will drive out
>   all the cattle;
> This noble captain yet was never known to fail us,
> But did the conquest get of all that did assail us;
> His furious rage none could assuage; but, to the world's
>   great wonder,
> He tears down banks and breaks their cranks and whirli-
>   gigs asunder.

To-day, when flood time comes on the washes it means a new food harvest for the birds. At this time of the year, when the flood waters from the uplands have spread in shallow seas over the meadows, the cattle marshes, and the peat

---

[1] It is an odd fact that when the Rev. Dr T. S. Whalley was presented by the Bishop of Ely to the living of Hagworthingham-in-the-Fens it was with the proviso that he should not live in the parish, as the air was fatal to any but a native.

land of the lowlands, the benefits are twofold. Man reaps one reward, the birds the other.

For the farmer's benefit the flooded meadows and marshes are enriched by a thick deposit of silt brought down from the uplands on the brown, discoloured waters of the flood. This top dressing of silt is better than any artificial manure. It is natural food for the earth—rich, real nourishment. These thousands of tons of disintegrated soil swept down from, let us say, Northamptonshire on to the flat fens of Cambridge-shire, are as valuable, in comparison, as a transfusion of blood from the strong to the weak.

It is the cheapest method of fertilization; the farmer pays nothing—except, perhaps, for a little ditching and draining to run the waters off later on.

But if the floods are of value to the farmer, they are a Heaven-sent blessing to the birds. For where there are floods there is food, food in abundance, just waiting to be picked up.

Almost every bird on the British list, from the golden eagle to the starling and the sparrow, welcomes the coming of floods. The eagle, soaring above the cavernous solitudes of a Highland corrie, empty alike of man and beast, sees far below him the tumbling silver streak of a mountain burn in full spate. The rivulet that yesterday was a mere thread of silver, this morning has swollen overnight, by some miracle, to a bold and over-leaping flood of waters, maned like a lion.

On the flood, tossing and bobbing, comes a pathetic woolly object, sodden and bulbous, looking rather like a saturated feather mattress—that inevitable victim of a Highland flood,

59

a drowned and foolish sheep. When, presently, it drifts in-shore and is stranded, the eagle swings lower and lower in tremendous half-mile wide arcs, until finally he is above the corpse. Then, with a sudden rush of sound, he plops on to the hard earth, cocks his head sideways at the dead sheep, hops clumsily a yard or two nearer, and the feast has begun.

The eagle is not alone. Out of the cold hollows of the hill comes the croak of the raven. The raven, with his great pick-axe of a beak, his bleak and murderous eye, steely in the plumage of death, joins the eagle at this feast of 'braxy' mutton the floods have provided.

And after, when the kings, gorged, have departed, there come those humbler scavengers, the carrion crow and hoodie, the great black-backed gull who barks over the sodden moor-land like a wandering dog, the rook and the jackdaw, and, last in the train of ghouls, the sly, sneaking, malevolent rat.

While these grim feasts of the Highland floods are taking place, other harvests come to the gentler birds of English meadows and valleys. Above the broad, shining sea of flood waters, perhaps three-quarters of a mile wide, which fill the valleys of Thames, Severn, Ouse, Arun, Medway, or Ribble, there sweep and tumble great flocks of green plover—blown cascades of black and white. One moment they sweep up to the skies in an ecstasy of light and movement. The next they tumble earthward, like autumn leaves.

No two birds fly or fall alike. They are masters of fantastic aerobatics.

Then, suddenly, the whole congregation—for that is the

medieval fowler's term—stream earthward in one flashing, falling torrent of silver undersides, swoop low over the water's edge, like a thousand shillings shot from a gun, and, as suddenly, drop motionless in a long line on the flood's brim.

There they stand like soldiers, all facing one way, each with his pert little crest erect, white-waistcoated, green-jacketed. For a moment they are poised, alert. Then as at a single word, they are running backward and forward, pecking here, pecking there, tripping daintily along the water's edge, wading shyly like young girls in the shallows. The floods have brought their harvest.

It is a harvest of drowned-out, washed-up slugs, beetles, worms, insects, and berries. Thousands of acres of low-lying grasslands have yielded their treasures of food. And the floods and a favourable wind have deposited this tremendous banquet at their doorstep.

To join the plover come starlings in their myriads, great banks of birds, tens of thousands strong, winging their way, direct, purposeful, across the apple-green and burnt gold of a winter sunset.

Linnets in their sober livery; chaffinches, pert and brilliant; magpies in black and white impudence; sparrows, fussy and invariably ill-mannered, push and jostle in the free-meal throng.

Farther out in the yard-deep waters, where lesser fry may not venture, one or two herons stalk like grey ghosts, pickers-up of small, bewildered fish, swallowers of frogs, snappers-up of drowned rats and dead mice. Anything that comes to a

61

heron's gullet in the shape of dead fish or fowl is good enough.

Snipe, those little, long-billed ballet dancers of the river-side meadows, grow fat on drowned-out worms. Rooks, gulls, crows, and jackdaws all take their toll.

SNIPE

Even the foxes come down at night—and sometimes by broad daylight—to prowl along the edge of the receding waters in search of flooded-out rabbits or hares arrested murderously as they swim ashore. Both hares and rabbits can swim for comparatively long distances. I have seen many a salt-marsh rabbit jump deliberately into a sea creek and swim five or ten yards athwart a four-knot tide.

Oddly enough, the only people who seem to be nonplussed by this new, sudden swelling of their native rivers are the ducks and the swans. Again and again, on the Thames in particular, you will see them being hurried down on the flood to within a few yards of destruction on the brink of some tumbling weir until, frightened by the roar of waters, they take wing and fly half a mile upstream again, merely to repeat the same stupid process a few minutes later.

But floods to them, as to almost every other bird, mean merciful deliverance from the starvation which inevitably follows prolonged frost.

SCAUP

II

As me and my companions were setting of a snare,
'Twas then we spied the gamekeeper—for him we
    did not care,
For we can wrestle and fight, my boys, and jump
    o'er anywhere.
Oh 'tis my delight on a shining night in the
    season of the year.
The Lincolnshire Poacher

Two gamekeepers were killed by poachers a few years ago. In the Midlands and the North, gangs of unemployed sweep the countryside with guns and dogs each week-end. No keeper dare face them.

A Cumberland landowner told me last year that in his district poaching is so widespread and the poachers so violent " that nothing short of an armed force could hold them up."

It all sounds like the ' hungry forties ' over again, a grim and sordid picture to contemplate. Yet as a lifelong poacher, tutored in its ancient arts in the heart of that magnificent game country of East Anglia, where I was born and bred, I deplore this new violence. My memories of poaching on the manors and marshes of home—some indeed were literally ' of home '—are different and more glamorous pictures.

We had more ways of taking a pheasant than by shooting him, Uriah and I. Uriah was the village poacher, bird-catcher, mole-trapper, eel-spearer, dyke-dydler, wildfowl-shooter, plover-netter, warrener, and rat-catcher.

Uriah—we were a Calvinistic village with Biblical names of singular ugliness as our sole sign of godliness—was, praise St Hubert, still is, a burly fellow with a North Sea face, black hair, black piercing eyes, and a hand like a ham. I liked him. I was ten then. I still like him.

Uriah wore a pilot coat of blue melton, bright brass buttons, velvet cords, waterboots, a moleskin waistcoat, and a seaman's peaked cap.

He had a gun, but he used it only on the river walls for duck. Pheasants we took in other and more ancient ways.

" Guns," said Ury, " guns is for gintlemen—or fools. I ain't none o' the both on 'em. I gits me buds natural." So let us take six illicit pheasants ' natural.'

Imagine then, if you will, a holt down on the edge of the fen—a choked acre of willow, poplar, and blackthorn bushes. Polecats lived there, a pair of them. Cat owls cried all night. The tall poplars shook in the autumn sun when no wind blew. They shivered through the still night. Otters crept in the reeds. Water-rails grunted and the great white barn owls screamed like banshees.

And up into the old blackthorns at night flew the pheasants, wily old cocks who dwelt in charmed security amid the sedges and rat runs of that wild, undrained fen which was my family heritage—a place of primeval beauty, untouched since Hereward's day. A sheer delight alloyed only by a ' drainage ' rate of twelve shillings an acre.

Into this dark holt on a winter night the infidels advance. One is burly and big. He carries a sack. The other is small

E   65

and full of desperateness. He bears, like an acolyte, a brazier and a wand. The brazier, to be meticulous, is a treacle tin half full of smouldering rags smothered in sulphur. The wand is a ten-foot bamboo, hollow throughout.

In the top of the treacle tin is a hole big enough to take the end of the bamboo. In the bottom and sides are ventilation holes.

Beneath a tall bush we pause. Above us, eight feet up, sits the bunched form of an old cock, limned blackly against the stars. The bamboo is fitted into the tin. The rags are blown into a blaze. The top of the pole is gently poked just under the sleeping pheasant's head.

In a few seconds the bird sways, lurches, pitches forward, and crashes through the branches to the ground. A twist of the neck and into the sack he goes. And so on to the next.

This, as you may observe, is an artist's job. No haste, no fuss, no pain, no blood, no noise, no lights, and no keeper any the wiser. Our best bag was fifteen in a night.

Uriah kept game bantams, fighting bundles of feathers that would challenge a Bengal tiger. They were half as big as a pheasant and twice as quick on their feet.

So, observe us on a Sunday morning, in a sunny ditch bottom on the southern side of the Church wood. Two bantam cocks are in the sack and the keeper is in church. His baby is being christened. So are the bantams.

Out comes the first cock. Steel spurs are put over his own and strapped to his legs and he is put down on the covert side. The change from dark to light is enough. Flapping his wings he crows a shrill challenge. Sunday morning, with the sun shining, is the time to fight the world. He crows again.

Back comes a challenge, a patter of feet on dead leaves and out from the yellowing brambles steps a grand old cock pheasant, all red and blue and jewelled like a pasha. One look at the little upstart whippersnapper who has sprung from nowhere is enough. This fellow cannot be tolerated for a moment.

The fight is short and moderately bloody. Side-stepping the pheasant the bantam springs into the air, one swift stroke of his glittering steel spurs and the pheasant's skull is split, the pheasant a wilted heap of colour.

It is a quick, clean death, and everything fit for the table. But I do not like it. A grand old cock pheasant, grand as a duke, should not die in such assassin's fashion. You might as well garotte an aristocrat of the old pre-beerage sort.

I think I prefer that ploughboy trick we had of making a dozen cones of thick brown paper, like ice-cream cones, smearing the inside edges with bird-lime, filling the bottoms with maize and then sticking them in the newly ploughed furrows just outside the covertside.

The pheasants were bound to come sneaking out for the worms and grubs, and equally bound to stick their beaks into the cones.

And then the cones stuck and half a dozen old cocks and hens would be tumbling wildly about, with April fools' caps stuck over their eyes, too blinded and too bewildered to fly. And Uriah and I would fill the sack again.

You can, of course, take your pheasants by salting their feeding-grounds with maize soaked in gin—they provide a perfect ' morning after ' police-court parade—or choke them with peas through which are threaded quarter-inch horsehairs. But that is a cad's trick.

The crude method of shooting them at roost is not to be recommended. In the first place, if the keeper has a sense of humour he will plaster the trees nearest the rides with wooden dummies. In the second place, the orthodox method of carrying a short-barrelled gun down the leg of one's trousers and trying to look like a wooden-legged sailor has its drawbacks. I know a man who tried it. The gun went off. He has a wooden leg now.

Finally, of course, these things, long suspected, leaked out at home, and an inquisition was held. For some days after I was in no fit state to pay calls, or indeed sit anywhere save on the most sympathetic air-cushions.

So after that the coverts and the pheasants were left alone and Uriah and I went to the marsh, which was no-man's-land and full of snipe, and broad, lazy dykes where the

III

THE SHOOTER to whom loneliness is abhorrent will never make a fowler. Indeed, one might go farther and say that he to whom loneliness is not refreshing, who does not feel exalted and uplifted by contact with desolation, had better stick to the company of his kind on moor and stubble.

HESKETH PRICHARD
Sport in Wildest Britain

How deep can a bird dive? How long can it remain under water? At what speed can it swim in such circumstances?

The man who can solve these three questions will answer a most remarkable triangular puzzle still confronting science.

He will, moreover, have furnished information which can very well be of the greatest assistance to the designers of the submarines of the future—for the study of birds has not only had a vital and far-reaching effect upon the development of modern aircraft, as witness the glider, the Heinkel light aeroplane, and the low-winged Monospar, all of which owe the essentials of their design to the essentials of wing construction in birds, but it is also believed that the structure of diving birds is the answer to the quest for the perfect submarine.

We may therefore study with real effect and to some definite purpose the actions of birds under water and the construction of those which can dive deepest and swim fastest. Knowledge on the subject is scanty. I have studied diving

73

ducks, grebes, divers of the *Colymbidae*, and auks on the coast for the past twelve years.

I have timed them from gunning punts, motor-boats, and fishing smacks, observing them at their normal business of seeking food and watching them also under stress of severe fright; that is, after they have been shot at.

These observations began some years ago at the instigation of the late Count de la Chapelle, and I owe much of the more detailed information available to the extremely erudite researches conducted by Dr J. M. Dewar.

Birds dive in various ways. Who that has ever seen a gannet plunge from the beetling crags of the Bass Rock and fall like a plummet into the sea in a spout of up-flung foam would imagine that so spectacular an entry into the ocean did not produce a dive as deep as that of some sober-plumaged, obscure little sea duck? One moment swimming calmly on the surface, the next, with a flick and a jump like a marine tumbler, the duck presents his posterior to the momentary gaze of heaven, and then, with rapid beats of his short, stumpy wings and grotesque little paddles, descends to twice or thrice the depth reached by that magnificent thunderbolt of snowy plumage which fell like a feathered rocket from the rock.

Actually, I do not believe that a gannet goes much deeper than thirty feet, while the velvet scoter certainly descends to sixteen fathoms, according to Boubier; and Horring says that the king eider can touch bottom in seventy-two fathoms of water.

This is a terrific depth, and one feels that it requires further and more detailed evidence and confirmation. Eider ducks have certainly been caught in nets set on the sea bottom thirty fathoms deep, and a Great Northern diver has been taken from a trammel net set at the same depth. There are plenty of such records, just as there are records of diving ducks caught on baited hooks set on the bottom at anything from ten to thirteen fathoms.

But, as Dr Dewar points out, we must remember that it takes a long time to haul a net to the surface, and the bird might well have been caught on the way up from the bottom. The same applies to a bird taken on a hook.

Hanna stated that he had taken crested auklets from the stomachs of cod caught two hundred feet deep. But here again the evidence is not sufficient. At what depth did the cod catch the birds? We cannot possibly say.

Personally, after watching a good many diving duck, some

EIDER DUCK

of which have been shot with freshly plucked seaweed in their beak when it was known that the weed grew at certain fixed depths, I have come to the conclusion that no bird goes much deeper than ten fathoms.

The scaup duck, which one can see diving in the London parks, seldom appear to go deeper than three fathoms, although so reliable an authority as Millais believed that they could reach eleven fathoms. The goldeneye probably dives to a depth of twenty feet and the surf scoter to twice that distance.

Cormorants do not, I think, dive as deeply as some of the diving ducks, while their speed under water is about half a mile in twenty minutes, or two feet per second. None of the diving ducks, with the possible exception of the mergansers, can travel at much more than a foot per second under water, but the great crested grebe, which can be timed any day on the Penn Ponds in Richmond Park, has been definitely proved to reach a speed of four feet a second under water without being in a particular hurry about it.

As for the amount of time which birds can spend under water, the velvet scoter holds the record with three minutes, followed by the Great Northern diver, the black-throated diver, and Cassin's auklet, all with two minutes each. These times were noted over periods during which the bird was not alarmed, but I have myself timed a tiny black-necked grebe at just over two minutes under water after it had been shot at and chased by a motor-boat.

The tufted duck and scaup both go down for about a

minute, according to Cordeaux and Millais, while Millais also timed the common pochard, the dunbird of the Essex fowlers, and Barrow's goldeneye both at a minute each, while the goosander, that lovely white pirate of the Scottish fisheries, can submerge for a full two minutes, during which time he will probably swallow a third of his own weight in fish.

So far the records show that the long stream-lined, bottle-necked birds with the powerful paddles and sharp-pointed, scythe-shaped wings can not only submerge the longest but swim the fastest and descend the deepest.

Here, then, is something for the submarine designers to think about. We have more to learn from birds than perhaps the engineers are yet prepared to admit.

MARCH

I

When I was a-reaping
  Near famed Wantage Town
A girt hare came leaping,
  So sleek an' so brown;
An' me being gifted,
  Like David, to sling,
A pebble I lifted
  An' dropped her at spring.

PATRICK CHALMERS
Green Days and Blue Days

IF you were to go, with an observant eye, into the country in a motor-car this week-end you would see tragedies and alarms, romances and excursions.

For this is the time of year when Nature, like the rest of the world, goes slightly mad.

Walk quietly down any little lane at the foot of a field of young spring wheat, where above you the upland meets the sky in a noble scarp, and you will see the mad March hares, more fantastic in their protestations than the newest propaganda from New Germany.

Over the sky-line they come cantering, with that ridiculous loppety-lop at which even rabbits laugh, ears cocked up, their slightly goat-like eyes blazing with the lights of love and battle. And when one jack hare meets another the result is ludicrous.

For they sit up on their hind quarters, cock their ears, and box with the bravado of a film boxer. Jack is there for the women who watch and cheer.

I do not know why it is, but at this time of the year the hare, who, normally, is an intelligent, fleet, and graceful creature, goes completely mad.

Had you walked down a field towards a hare a month ago he would have been up and off like a streak of light. To-day it is ten to one that he will come cantering towards you, in a stupid and abstract fashion, so myopic that the artful farm labourer will sometimes stand still and kill him with a quick swipe of a shovel. For it is an odd thing that when hares are running forward they look backward, particularly if chased. And usually they run in a wide circle.

Rabbits in their courtship are more lively, less stupid, and

mongoose. Nothing waited when the mongoose went in. We once bolted three foxes in an afternoon that way, put them in a bag, and sold them to a huntsman at Bishop's Stortford. That made my week's pocket-money.

WEASEL

IV

Old songs that sung themselves to me,
  Sweet through a boy's day-dream,
While trout below the blossom'd tree
  Plashed in the golden stream.

ANDREW LANG

Three of the most striking birds in the whole bird world
have just arrived in England, and are busy house-hunting.
Each of the three—the cuckoo, the swallow, and the willow
wren—has more character and individuality than many a
human being.

We will talk first of the willow wren, that small and
humble creature, shy as a maiden, lowly in its habitation,
gentle in its song, so indistinguished in its dress that if you
are no student of birds it will look almost exactly like any
one of half a dozen other quiet little birds, brown and
mouselike, who go about their daily business, unconsidered
trifles of the hedgerows. Its nest is built near the ground,
hidden at the bottom of some bush or straggling hedgerow,
perhaps overhanging the lip of a ditch where the brambles
creep out into the field—or tucked away low down at the
base of an old apple-tree.

The nest itself is tiny and soft, made of moss and fine
grasses with perhaps horsehair, sheep's wool, rabbit's fur,
bits of string, and any other oddments worked into it so that
the chicks may live the days of their youth in a chamber

soft almost as silk. It has a door at the side just like the nest of a jenny wren. There are five to eight eggs, white, with light red to purplish red spots. But to find this nest you must have eyes sharp as a stoat's, the acute bird's-nesting nose of a schoolboy. Its placing and its materials are among the marvels of camouflage in Nature.

The mother bird, creeping like a silent, eager little mouse through the undergrowth, is a dynamo in miniature, one of the most amazing examples of potted energy.

From the first light of dawn she is feeding her young. Their appetites are beyond belief.

Most of their food is small caterpillars and aphides. Mr T. Hyde-Parker, who watched a pair of these birds from before five o'clock in the morning until after nine o'clock the same evening, has recorded that during that time the parents fed the young at the rate of approximately five caterpillars to every six minutes! Work that out and then imagine how many caterpillars must have been devoured by the family during the day. If you are a gardener you will agree that the willow wren deserves canonization.

There is scarcely a part of Europe where the willow wren is not found, and during the spring and summer months, when it comes to us from over the Channel, it is easily one of our commonest migrants. But when autumn comes it leaves us, flies to the South of France and Spain, crosses the Mediterranean, conquers the Sahara by some unknown wizardry of its own, and penetrates the continent of Africa as far south as the thirtieth degree of latitude.

With the willow wren comes the cuckoo, but I cannot find it in my heart to regard the cuckoo with the same benevolent eye. The old country belief that the cuckoo disguised itself as a hawk in winter time in order that it might then prey upon and eat the little birds which had been its foster-parents during the spring is a pretty bit of cynicism, not in the least undeserved. For the cuckoo's life in this country is one long history of burglary, robbery, murder, and general black-guardism.

Before a hen cuckoo decides to inflict her egg upon some hapless small bird——be it hedge-sparrow, meadow pipit, or sedge warbler——she will trail the mother bird for an hour or more with all the cunning of a Sherlock Holmes, the persistence of a bloodhound. Once she has located the nest and decided that the foster-parents will do, she proceeds with her egg-laying.

While the business of taking temporary possession of the nest is going on the rightful owners do all in their power to resist and drive the cuckoo away. The effect on the cuckoo is *nil*. She just goes blandly on with her business.

The moment the egg is deposited she leaves. Now it is a very odd fact that although the foster-parents up to this very moment have shown the strongest and most vocal dislike to this addition to their family, the instant the egg is there they take it as their own. It usually hatches out about a fortnight later.

Within a few hours the young cuckoo, although still blind, has grown sufficiently large and strong to be able to put the other youngsters out of the nest. He does this by burrowing under them, heaving them on to his back and then shuffling to the edge of the nest, where he tips them over, either to be killed by the fall or to die of exposure. Within a very few hours he has cleared the nest of the lot. From that time onward the wretched hedge-sparrows, pipits, or sedge warblers who may be his foster-parents become his slaves. Their lives, until he is big enough to fly, are one unending drudgery of providing food for the great, gaping bully who has murdered their young.

It is a strange and notable fact, by the way, that if a human being places a cuckoo's egg in a nest the birds will throw it out. But if the cuckoo puts it there it immediately becomes their first duty and concern.

I have a greater love for that third of our trinity of 'individuals,' the swallow.

The swallow flies between two and three thousand miles, from the heart of Africa to the heart of England, in order to produce his young under the English sun. Year after year he comes back to the same farmhouse eaves, the same village church tower, which, perhaps, was built when James I was racing his horses at Newmarket.

By what extraordinary instinct the swallows are able to follow the immemorial air lines from the shore of, shall we say, Victoria Nyanza, to the walls of some old farmhouse in a sleepy English village is more than the wit and knowledge of man can explain. We shall probably never know. But year by year they return.

APRIL

I

The chaffinch that builds in a scarecrow betrays
    A legitimate taste for variety.
The titmouse that nests by a sister displays
    A praiseworthy love of society.

The robins may build where their whim shall advise,
    And be guilty of no impropriety.
If larks did the same, you would open your eyes
    And declare that they sought notoriety.

               E. D. CUMING
              Idlings in Arcadia

IF you go into the country on any windy morning of early spring you will see a stirring of birds about the tree-tops, an activity unwonted during the stark months of winter. The rooks show it most of all. For they are a gregarious, noisy, demonstrative lot, uncareful of their private affairs. What goes on goes on and they don't care a hang who sees.

So we will see the black wind-blown scouts sitting unsteadily on tossing branches, cawing above the gusty revel of the wind. They swing and peer, pry and scramble among the ragged wrecks of last year's nests. It goes on most of the day.

But at night they still gather in their thousands in the old pasture field, acres of busy gabbling black bodies which presently rise up and fly in ragged cohorts against the disordered beauty of the sunset to the ancient wood which is their dormitory. But the sleeping wood of winter is not the rookery of summer, the place where nests are built, eggs are laid and the young are hatched and fed.

But the urge to build is on them. Hence this scrambling about during the day in the topmost branches of the rook trees, this clatter, noise, and inquisitiveness. Soon they will begin to build. And when the tree-tops which now are black, bleak and bare, break into a sea of misty green the rooks will be sitting and another year of housekeeping will have begun.

And if you go down on to the marsh where the reeds stand withered and dead in peat-stained dykes, on to the windy levels where the bullocks move in humped, uneven lines, like bison on a forgotten prairie, you will see that even the heron who stand by day, solemn, immobile fishermen of philosophy, even they have taken on a new and gay skittishness. They are about in pairs instead of the ' sieges ' of half a dozen or more which one met only a month ago fishing on the tide line.

And there on the marshes, below the sea walls where soon the cuckoo-flowers will bud and the kingcups will star the dyke banks with sudden brassy flecks of gold, the wild duck have already paired.

The whole bird world is thinking of nesting. The gun is oiled and put away. The fowler's sea boots are stuffed with hay and hung up to dry. The old retriever blinks her eyes before the fire at night and twitches in dreams of past hunting. There is peace among the birds.

Now why does the rook, like the heron, build a ragged

nest of sticks and twigs in the windy top of a tall tree where
the gales may roar about his wife, while the wild duck nests
inconspicuously among the sedges on a damp and muddy
floor? And why, you may ask equally, does the magpie build

MAGPIE

in wary solitude in the top of a wind-twisted thorn, putting
a roof of twigs above his nest, while the little wren creeps
like a silent mouse into the lowliest hedge bottom, there to
build a tiny nest, the most delicate thing you ever saw, walled
and roofed with green moss, horsehair, sharp grasses, a little
round ball with a door at the side, scarcely large enough for
a man to thrust in his thumb?

Here are minor mysteries. They are part of the everyday
astonishing lives of the birds. And if you walk across a bare

107

ploughed field and come miraculously upon a clutch of plovers' eggs, invisible almost to the eye yet laid only on the bare earth, you may ask equally why one bird should build high in the cathedral of the tree-tops while this other, the plover, that acrobat of the skies, should come down like the skylark to nest on the cold and bitter earth.

There is a reason for all these things. The rook and the heron build high and in colonies because at the time of mating they are friendly and gregarious people, fond of each other's company, wary of men. From the tall tree-tops they can spy the raider from below. By sheer force of numbers they can defeat the raider from above. And the very insecurity of their nesting places is an insurance against small boys who climb hazardously. There is wisdom in their loftiness of architecture.

But the magpie is a solitary creature, a robber of other birds' nests, an outcast and a villain. So he nests high in thin branches where men cannot reach him. But he puts a roof of twigs over his nest so that neither rook nor gull may easily raid his eggs in revenge for the magpie's depredations on their own. But if you look closely at the magpie's untidy home you will see that he builds it not only with a door by which he may go in at one side but with another by which he may retreat on the other. The reason is twofold, but the main and first reason is that the magpie's wife has a long tail, so that when she sits on her eggs her beak and watchful eyes guard the entry while her tail sticks out of the back door.

The little mouse-like wren has no need of these back-door tricks. Once in her snug, tiny home her little cocked-up tail fits in perfectly. She is warm, protected, invisible.

As for the wild duck, if you squelch noisily along the wet margin of mere or dyke she will crouch flat, her brown back all of an exact piece in colouring with the streaked and withered sedges about her. She makes little or no nest beyond the down plucked from her own breast. And when she slips, snakelike, off her eggs, the down is pulled over the eggs to keep them warm. Sometimes, even a few dead, sodden, rushes are raked across the heap to complete the camouflage.

As for the peewit, the stone curlew, or the little ringed plover who pipes up the lonely ditches, these need to make no nests at all, for their eggs and their plumage blend perfectly with their surroundings. To build a nest will be merely to challenge attention.

In fact, it is an odd but even contestible fact that among nearly all birds which nest in the open the female is more inconspicuously coloured than the male. She must be in the nature of things, for her most dangerous time of life is when she is sitting on her nest. On her freedom from discovery depends the safety not only of herself but of her family. The hen blackbird, the female chaffinch, the hen pheasant, the partridge and the wild duck are all cases in point.

And when you find a bird which nests in the open but is none the less brightly coloured, the brightness is always underneath where its colours will be hidden from view while

109

the bird is sitting. The red waistcoat of the robin, the pure white underparts of the green plover and the speckled breast of the thrush are everyday examples.

But the kingfisher, who is a jewel in colours, goes out of sight altogether when he seeks a nest. Like the shell-duck, whose brilliant chestnut and white make them the handsomest duck on British waters, they seek safety for their young by nesting in holes. The kingfisher goes deep into a hole in the bank where his mate and her pure white eggs are invisible. The shell-duck takes possession of a rabbit burrow. Equally, the green woodpecker, the brightly coloured tits, and the nuthatch all go into holes, while the owl seeks the dark solitude of a hollow tree where the bright light of day cannot dazzle the eyes of his mate.

There is a rule in Nature that everything should be as beautiful and brightly coloured as possible, which is why the eggs of most birds which nest in trees or bushes are streaked, blotched, and mottled in greens, blues, blacks, reds, and browns. But if you look at their eggs with the shifting sunlight dappled on them through the branches you will discover that the arts of camouflage were no new thing when mankind tardily discovered them in time of war. The wisdom of birds, their old, old mysteries of flight, their protective coloration and their astonishing architectures are older in elements of knowledge than all our new sciences of aviation, camouflage, and building.

II

Indeed, wherever I may go,
    Through summer woods, by wintry fell,
I've found you, in the sun or snow,
    A friendly little Ishmael.
                    PATRICK CHALMERS
                    Green Days and Blue Days

Suddenly down the trunk of the nearest beech in the wood where I stood there scampered a swift and furry thing. Silvery blue-grey on the back, with a bright chestnut brush, ear-tufts that stood up in the most ridiculous fashion, and big round eyes; then he stopped like a shot.

A second before he had seemed to slide rather than scamper down its glass-smooth trunk—a streak of movement. And now there he sat, immobile, erect on his haunches, ears and ear-tufts perkily erect, his tail curled up over his back in perfect symmetry, his forepaws primly folded on a beech nut clasped to his bosom. And thus he sat, while I stood. For an enormous sixty seconds we looked at each other. Finally, convinced that I was made of wood, he began to dig. A swift and slovenly scrabbling, an inch or two deep—and the nut was deposited in its little grave, the earth scraped back again.

For a second he stood poised again, watching me. Then up the trunk like a flash, out along a branch in a breath— and suddenly—flat. He flattened to invisibility. His whole

III

body seemed to melt into the branch. He became part of the tree. But all the time those bright beady eyes were watching. Had I for a moment shifted my gaze it would have been difficult to have picked him up again.

For seven minutes he stayed there. Then, far away, the sound of a horn came on the damp air. In a flash he was off, racing through the tree-tops like a fury of fur.

Squirrels do these odd things in autumn and winter. Some

RED SQUIRREL

be such a slave or a fool as to feed them until they are full winged, fit to fly.

How then will they reach the water? For I cannot imagine that she will turn them out brutally to fall with a flop, which

"Fish-hawk"

might quite easily mean death, into the water beneath. That is the question which my friend is asking himself. As some sort of a godfather in this matter, he is quite properly anxious. But I have assured him that the mother duck, when her young are little more than balls of down, will take them one by one on her back and plane down gently to the surface of the moat, like a seaplane alighting with its passengers. An old man on the farm says that he has twice seen a duck do this when she has nested in a tree.

And why not? After all, a tree is no place for a duck

to nest, although mother ducks are of an adventurous turn of mind and do so on rare occasions.

But then mother birds have the oddest ways of transporting their young to safety. For example, there was a long and historic controversy—it raged for quite seventy years—as to whether the woodcock carried its young between its thighs when flighting from one part of its home wood to another. Letters on this subject appeared in the leading sporting journals and *The Times* from 1870 onward. Various well-known sportsmen and naturalists, including the late Sir Ralph Payne-Gallwey and the sixth Lord Walsingham, the best shot that ever lived, quoted keepers and woodsmen who said that they had seen it. The museum naturalists and scientists scoffed at them. But to-day it is an accepted fact.

The woodcock, that graceful creature with the beak of a snipe, the flight of an owl, the large liquid eyes that are peculiarly its own, and the beautiful barred and mottled plumage which harmonizes so perfectly with fallen autumn leaves that you may almost tread on the bird before you see it—this very individual bird, the most coveted trophy in the shooting world, is a perfect and devoted mother.

At this time of the year she nests on heathery hillsides, on the bracken-covered slopes of old parks, among the fern and fallen leaves in the quiet corners of ancient woods where the squirrels scamper and the jays chatter impudently. And when dusk falls and the woodcock goes forth to feed in swampy hollows and by the shores of little marshy pools she carries her young with her, a little long-beaked, round-eyed

" The most coveted trophy in the shooting world."

ball of fluff nipped firmly and comfortably between the mother's thighs.

Major J. W. Seigne, who is probably the greatest living authority on snipe and woodcock, has a sanctuary for these birds on his estate near Thomastown, in Ireland. And writing to me recently he said: " I have seen a woodcock carry its young not once but many times. The last one passed over my head not more than ten feet up. It flew straight with a noiseless owl-like flight, rather like a big moth coming at me out of the wood. Once or twice it emitted a low, distinct croak. I could see the young bird quite clearly held between the parent bird's thighs. Those who dispute that this bird carries its young in this manner are quite wrong. I waited for years before I could see it and now, in the last two seasons, I have seen it not once but several times."

There is first-hand evidence from a patient and first-class observer. And why not? The swan will sail serenely about a pool with its newly hatched young nestling comfortably in the feathers on its back. Old country people will tell you that when parent ducks rear their young on a pool infested with hungry pike, only too ready to gobble up the newly hatched duckling, that the mother bird sometimes sails over the deep pools where the pike lurk with her young squatting safely on her back until they reach the security of the shallows.

But there are other birds which do far more than merely carry their young. There are the big birds, the crane and the great eagle owl which the peasants of northern Europe swear carry the tiny golden-crested wren, a little jewel of a bird no larger than half a crown, safely tucked away among the feathers on their backs, on voyages across hundreds of miles of swamp and sea, pine forest and northern waste.

There have been no cranes in England, as regular visitors, for the last two hundred years. But the fishermen and fowlers of the north-east coast firmly believe that the big wood owls which drift in from the North Sea, over hundreds of miles of wintry waters from Norway and Sweden, bear the tiny wrens upon their backs as stowaways. It is a charming thought, and you will find its root a thousand years back in the folklore and superstitions of Scandinavia and the North.

Most bird mothers take infinite pains not only to protect their young when helpless, but to teach them how to fly when semi-fledged. I have seen a rook push its squawking youngster out of the nest and guide it among the swaying twigs in a tree-top sixty dizzy feet above the earth. I have seen young herons swinging and scrambling like cats in the tops of swaying elms while the parent birds peered and hovered anxiously. Watch a moorhen leading her flotilla of little black balls about the surface of the lake in St James's Park—tiny midgets that swim with amazing celerity, seeming to scutter across the surface like water beetles.

Observe a partridge, when you have surprised her young at a dust bath in the ruts of some lonely country lane. See how she flutters helplessly up the lane in front of you, appearing to be broken winged, incapable of escape, easy

I

THE PALE BLUE of the upper sky faded into clear emerald green, this into primrose, then into orange and deep crimson red, while below stretched the steely indigo of the sea. It seemed as if a mighty rainbow, straight instead of curved, lay along the horizon. On our left the purple brownness of the bog stretched itself away in level mysterious miles.

GILFRID W. HARTLEY
Wild Sport and Some Stories

THE smell of the sea is strong to-night here on the marsh where the landward trees stand black, a far frieze against the sunset. The marsh lies between the sea and the uplands, a triangle of brilliant green, seared by the rust of reedy dykes, splashed by the silver of fleets and long marsh pools.

On one side is the river, the lonely estuary that sweeps ten miles into the land, two miles wide, with no town upon its bank, no yacht upon its waters. On the other is ' the channel,' the home channel where the shrimpers lie at anchor and the smacks dry their nets against the sun. And at the nose of the marsh, at the ' Naas,' as they still call it in the Danish of far-off days, is the sea, old and empty and wide.

Behind all these lie the Essex elms and the old Essex farms, yellow-walled and moated, the farms with their lands that are blood and bone of English history.

There is no trackway upon the marsh and no man. It is green and rough with thistles, cut by dykes, a place of

125

rabbits and redshank, where the shoveller nest and the snipe drum.

Water gleams in the green here and there as a fleet shows suddenly, a dyke shines like a sword. The cattle are distant humps, giant molehills. Not until you look at them do you realize the distance and breadth of the marsh.

Outside the sea wall the saltings meet the mud and the tide sucks and gurgles. The muds are bare and the long green widgeon grass smells salt and strong. What memories that salt smell wakes of bitter winter nights and white dawns when the black geese cackled on the sand banks and the widgeon swung overhead in thousands, bitter nights in the punt, white dawns in a gut in the salts, waiting for the flight when all the world was asleep.

Rooks flap up the tide line and the gulls scream as they dip and swing. The last curlew of all the great herds of winter rises and goes shrieking down the wall—a misanthrope who will remain all summer when he, by all his rights, should be whistling on the hills of Galloway. It is almost warm here in the glow of evening—or does one merely fancy that because the red of the sunset on the tide burns up the masts of the smacks, smoulders in their drying nets and turns them to fire. Sixteen small ships on fire, with masts and cordage burnt out in black against a Hobbema sky.

There is a stillness in the marshes like no other quiet in any other place—the stillness of empty sea and open sky, of a chorus of birds and no man's voice. This stillness takes no heed of such things as the drumming of a snipe, the lowing of bullocks, the bell-like piping of the redshank, and the rush of the terrier through the sea-wall grass. They are potent sounds, an emphasizing part of the silence. The birds and the cattle and the suck of the tide, and the lift of the yellow moon above the sea—these are spring.

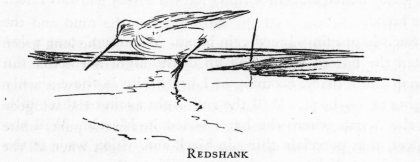

REDSHANK

Ceaselessly, far into the night, the redshank will pipe and flute, swinging slow in circles over the wall, hovering on swift fluttering wings, settling on the saltings, starting up again like arrows. They are the most restless birds on all the tide. Even the peewits who weep and wail and flock overhead in that queer, heavy, round-winged flight which is theirs in spring are not so tireless as these 'tukies' of the flats.

Somewhere, by the edge of the great fleet where the eels run to pounds in weight and will bite through a man's boot, a heron cries harshly, *fraa-ank! fraa-ank!*—he has seen the dog, and he lifts, black and ragged against the sunset-stained waters, to beat slowly away over the marsh, a Valkyriean figure in the dusk.

Down on the tide-line a sheldrake laughs with that ghostly

127

laugh which was half the mystery of those winter nights afloat. His mate is nesting up in the rabbit holes on the marsh. Each year they increase, like the shoveller and the tufted duck. Before long there will be nobler fowl nesting on the marsh, if these things are a sign to read. Last year a garganey nested and three times has the lovely gadwall raised her brood.

Such happenings breed vain hopes. Will there come a day when the bittern will swing up in the night sky above the marsh and estuary, booming as I heard him in those ghostly nights of boyhood? Will the ruff fight again on those hills in the marsh where the hares boxed in March? Will the avocet, that porcelain thing in black and white, wade in the broad fleets, flicker over the dykes? These things may come. May I be there to see them.

A 'Maybird' titters up the fleet side, and from high up in the green and blue of the evening sky comes that clear answering whistle which is the very spirit of the salt levels. Fifteen of them, strung out in a straggling V, beating on, high over the marsh, in a purposeful line for that other and greater marsh, the best in all Essex, where the fleets are wide and silent, the reed beds are deep, the old decoy gleams, and the gulls quarrel at their nesting. You may know that these whimbrel, the 'Maybirds' of Essex, the 'half jacks' of Norfolk, have come from far by that high, V-shaped flight, that purposeful direction. They will drop presently in Penny-hole Bottom and there wash off the mud of Spain or the white salt brine of the Zuider Zee.

"Down on the tide-line."

JUNE

OBSERVATION is the most enduring of the pleasures of life.
GEORGE MEREDITH
Diana of the Crossways

GOLDEN PLOVER flying at eighty miles an hour . . .
elephants stampeding at half a mile a minute . . .
salmon migrating at twenty-five miles a day . . . the giant
tunny flashing through the water at perhaps forty-five miles
an hour. No field of speculation could be wider or more
fascinating.

Our exact knowledge of the speed at which birds, animals,
and fish can travel without the fortuitous aids of wind and
tide are sketchy and far from complete. Bird speeds have
been worked out to a certain extent, but much remains to be
discovered. We have a working basis to go upon, but no exact
formula.

Animal speeds are in that fascinating state of conjectural
possibilities where one man's knowledge of one particular
species is probably governed by local conditions and cannot be
regarded as more than a contributory unit to the general
solution of the question. For instance, buffalo or elephant
may be capable of much higher average speeds in one part of
the world than in another, according to local conditions of
soil and general ' going.'

As for fish, we know practically nothing definite, although

139

that painstaking authority Mr W. L. Calderwood, of the Scottish Board of Fisheries, is hard at work investigating the subject.

The whole question, more particularly with regard to birds and fish, opens up an immense field for research, the results of which may well have the most profound bearing on the future design of aircraft, submarines, and high-speed motor vessels.

The late Sir Henry Segrave, a very dear friend, told me when he was designing the Segrave " Meteor," the most perfectly streamlined aeroplane of its type, that he was certain that if we could determine the aerodynamics of a bird in flight and ascertain the exact wind resistance of its feathers, we should be able to build the perfect, fool-proof aeroplane.

Since then the growth of gliding has shown that motorless flight follows precisely the principles employed by birds when they make use of air-currents and up-draughts. Watch gulls flying about cliffs, or other birds approaching and topping the steep wall and roof-tree of a house. Inevitably there is a flattening-out of the wings at the moment of approach, a sudden sweep upward and an effortless swing over the cliff or the house. That guiding spirit behind modern civil aviation, Lord Sempill, spends half his holidays at the Lizard watching the behaviour of gulls, guillemots, and terns in the wind eddies and currents off those tremendous cliffs.

Fortunately, a good deal has been done in the last few years to fix a more or less reliable average table of speeds for quite a number of British birds, the value of which cannot be

A June Idyll

exaggerated either to the designers of aircraft or to the man who shoots and wants to know how much forward allowance he should give.

I am indebted to Major H. J. Eley of Imperial Chemical Industries for many of the following estimates of the speeds of various birds. Some of these speeds were arrived at by the firm's experts after an exhaustive series of wind-tunnel and other tests. Others have been contributed by reliable observers to the *Shooting Times*, *Field*, etc. I am also personally indebted to the late Sir Henry Segrave, Sir Malcolm Campbell, Lord Sempill, and Captain David Wolfe-Murray for other estimates.

Practically all the speeds shown in the following table may definitely be taken as the maximum of which the particular birds were capable, as, in every case, the observer was either in an aeroplane or car or watching a bird pursued by a hawk —and therefore going at top speed.

All these birds were labouring under severe fright, and their speeds are therefore valuable only as indications of the maximum they are capable of. Some years ago a Mr Griffiths, of the Schultze Gunpowder Company, tried some experiments with a pheasant which he flew down a tunnel and timed. I believe the average speed worked out at 47 m.p.h., which is probably a little in excess of the speed at which the bird would fly under normal conditions. If we were to put the average driven pheasant's speed on a windless day at 40 m.p.h. I do not think one would be far wrong.

For all practical purposes of these estimates I am assuming

that the speed should be arrived at under the following conditions: (*a*) over a comparatively short distance—short, that is, according to the normal length of the bird's flight; (*b*) horizontal flight; (*c*) the bird to be flying normally and without alarm; (*d*) windlessness.

Obviously these are the ideal conditions and, equally obviously, the bulk of the estimates have been arrived at under different conditions, usually when the birds were frightened by aircraft or hawks. But taking a general average from the mass of opinions which I have collected during the past ten years, I should say that the following table of average speeds under the conditions outlined above is not far wrong.

	M.P.H.		M.P.H.
Golden Plover	45–50	Partridge	33–36
Teal	45–50	Green Plover	30
Blackcock	50	Jackdaw, Rook,	
Peregrine (when not		Wood Pigeon	30–33
stooping)	50	Kestrel	30–33
Pheasant	40	Goose	35–40
Grouse	40	Swan	35
Mallard	40–45	Heron	35–38
Merlin	40	Swallow	30
Blue Rock	40	Swift	45–50

Why or how anyone should have bothered to time that singularly unlovely flier, the landrail, is beyond my comprehension. In any case, I very much doubt if either the landrail, moorhen, or coot can average more than 20 m.p.h. in normal flight, although all three can fly fast and high when thoroughly disturbed, as those who have attended the annual coot shoots at Hickling, Abbotsbury, and elsewhere know to their unconfessed shame.

One useful result of these investigations has been the establishment of certain basic principles which have a definite value from the point of view of aircraft construction. For example, it has been proved that it is not the wing area which determines the speed at which a bird can fly, but the wing area and structure in relation to the weight of the bird. It is almost certainly correct to say that a heavy bird can fly faster than a lighter bird of the same type.

For instance, a capercailzie hen will generally fly faster than a grey hen, a grey hen faster than a grouse, and a grouse faster than a partridge.

The speed of the wing beat is most deceptive. How often has one seen a flapping, apparently slow-moving, blackcock overtake and pass a pack of grouse which, with their quick wing beats, appeared to be travelling much faster?

It will be noticed that nothing has been said of the speed of snipe, woodcock, and quail. This is because their inherent habit of twisting at what seems lightning speed makes accurate observation almost impossible.

Personally, I regard teal, golden plover, and herons as the most fascinating British birds to study in relation to speeds— the first two because they are so very fast, the third because he is so exceptionally deceptive as he flaps along.

A teal, as he suddenly shoots out of the dusk, twists overhead, and then dives downward like a streak of light, is surely the most difficult shot ever presented by that most difficult form of shooting—flighting. I have seen teal pass overhead, after they had been shot at, at speeds which seemed utterly incredible.

That excellent, if somewhat intolerantly self-opinionated authority on wildfowling, the late Sir Ralph Payne-Gallwey,

TEAL

says in one volume of his *Letters to Young Shooters* that he had actually timed teal passing between one headland and another at a hundred and twenty miles an hour! I am not sure that I can believe it . . . unless there was a strong following wind.

With regard to the speed of animals, the field of knowledge is more restricted, although one would have thought that computation would have been easier. The real reason is that nowadays birds are of more practical value as objects of study for students of aerodynamics. Who cares at what speed

Mr Frohawk's general conclusion is that pike under such circumstances of acute terror can move at probably fifteen miles an hour, possibly more, for a short distance. Other coarse fish, owing to their inferior 'stream-lining,' are several miles slower, while the trout when scared does not, in all probability, exceed twelve miles an hour.

One of these days someone, probably Mr Calderwood, will study fish speeds in a large glass tank with an efficient speed-recording apparatus. Then the naval architects will revive from that long sleep in which they have been enveloped since the *Mauretania* took the water over twenty years ago, and we shall be given a ship capable of a real advance in speed.

At present the super-modern *Bremen* is only a fraction faster than the aged *Mauretania*! Shipbuilding design has gone girlish over tennis courts, cocktail bars, dance floors, swimming baths, and modernistic state rooms; while other nations capture our seaborne trade—and the fish are waiting with the answer to the whole problem.

JULY

I

He clasps the crag with crooked hands;
Close to the sun in lonely lands,
Ring'd with the azure world, he stands.

The wrinkled sea beneath him crawls;
He watches from his mountain walls,
And like a thunderbolt he falls.

LORD TENNYSON
The Eagle

NOT long ago a citizen, walking through Highgate Woods in the evening, was startled to find his undistinguished hat snatched from his head by a sudden apparition which emitted the most blood-curdling scream. This citizen, you will not be surprised to learn, was momentarily so terrified that he jumped a yard. And then his hat fell from the air. A large bird, ghostly white and saffron yellow, swept through the darkening trees on noiseless wing. Slightly shaken, the citizen picked up the undistinguished hat and returned to the safety of bricks and mortar to spread the panic news. Some said it was a ghost, others an eagle, and others a monstrous owl, a ghoul with a murderous hatred of humanity.

The truth is it was just an ordinary barn owl on the look out for food for her newly hatched youngsters. Anything that looked brown and moved was good enough to pick up. But when she found that the hat was empty of all save a jumping human being she naturally screamed in her fright and dropped it. But I am quite certain that that orthodox citizen of Highgate is convinced that he was deliberately attacked, with murderous intent, by a highly dangerous creature.

It is very odd how little we know about British birds of prey, that is, the ordinary everyday ones, and the ridiculous misconceptions of humans from which they suffer. Birds of prey, like old ladies who support anti-sport campaigns and keep cats which catch mice, like a little piece of meat for their dinner or an egg with their tea. But that is no reason why we should condemn them utterly nor persecute them thoughtlessly.

For one thing, our birds of prey, our hawks and owls, are among the noblest, most beautiful, and most romantic of all the birds in Britain. They are buccaneers of the air, bandits with every man's hand against them, privateers with a licence to kill and a gun waiting for them at the corner of every wood.

But when you go into the country this week-end, forget for once the lowlier and gentler birds, the blackbirds and thrushes, the christian little robins who will fight to the death with a bloodthirstiness unbelievable; the brilliant, swaggering starlings, those enchanting mocking birds who make holes in your thatched roof and bully the swallows out of their nests. Forget the graceful swans who murder little ducklings by drowning them; forgo watching the graceful movements of those tiny appealing little shrew mice who,

"On moorlands there is the merlin."

when they fight, do so with such fury that they die of heart attacks and then are eaten by their opponents.

Forget these creatures who in nine cases out of ten enjoy a fictitious reputation for beauty and gentleness, and regard the hawks. There are the kestrel and the sparrow-hawks,

PEREGRINE

both common anywhere. On moorlands there is the merlin, a little jewel in grace of flight by the high cliffs, and on the bold hills of the North Country the peregrine stoops on his prey, a rushing thunderbolt of feathers, at eighty miles an hour.

The hobby, the fastest falcon of them all, would catch and kill a full-grown swift or swallow in full flight without pausing for an instant in its giddy rush. And if you climb up to a hobby's nest, although the female is no larger than your fist, she will sit there defiant, unblinking, unafraid. And if you dare to touch her young she will be on you in a flash, like a rocket, lifting miraculously just at the moment when you expect her to strike your head like a bullet. But she will leave behind talon marks where no hair will grow. I know, for my friend, Captain C. W. R. Knight, the man who first trained a golden eagle to fly at hares, who you will remember made that wonderful film of his tame eagle Mr Ramshaw, is marked to this very day by the talons of an indignant hobby. The man who tamed the eagle was driven from the tree-tops by almost the smallest falcon in the whole tribe.

But because the hawks and owls live by catching their prey on the wing, because every now and then while we are walking or motoring we see them chase and kill the small birds, it does not mean that they are necessarily doing a great deal of damage.

Fifty years ago every gamekeeper on every big estate had orders to kill any bird of prey at sight. The result was that jackdaws, rooks, rats, snakes, and all sorts of creatures which in their way can do a great deal of damage to agriculture, poultry, orchards, and game, flourished and increased unchecked by their natural enemies.

To-day we have discovered that the noble pirates of the air—or at any rate some of them—may well be the greatest friends of man. The barn owl, that lovely ghost-like wraith of white and saffron-yellow who snatched off the hat of the man in Highgate Woods, is worth his weight in gold as a rat killer. The brown wood owl beats up the hedges and over the fields, round the stackyards where the rats creep and the mice run in scores. Between them these two kill far more rats—the one animal for whom no sort of excuse for existence can be made—than all the traps and poisons put together.

156

The kestrel, that graceful hawk whom you will see hovering on fluttering wings any day over almost any cornfield—the windhover of the old countryman, a lovely name—is hovering in the wind merely because he is watching not so much for young partridges as for mice, voles and shrews, beetles and snakes.

Take a nobler creature, the peregrine falcon. I know a man who owns a grouse moor. A pair of peregrines nested in one of his cliffs. He swore that they killed eight hundred grouse a year so his keeper exterminated them. And the jackdaws took possession of that cliff-face instead. And week by week, day by day, throughout the breeding season you might see two hundred or more jackdaws beating that moor like setter dogs. Every jackdaw meant a grouse nest robbed of its eggs. Finally, my friend saw sense. He allowed a pair of peregrines to return. They nested undisturbed. And now there are not more than twenty couple of jackdaws on the whole of that moor. And when we climbed up to the peregrines' nest we found more bones of rats, rabbits, and small birds than we did of grouse.

So you see there is a great deal of beauty in these lovely creatures which live by the old, old rule of piracy and brigandage, which exists by swiftness and strength, which give grace to their surroundings and ride the winds for their living. Theirs is beauty and a certain nobility. They give us a glimpse of adventure, of the old high ideals of courage and dash. And they are by no means so black or so bloody as they are painted.

it vigorously, spitting out the poison every now and then. If you are by water where leeches abound, put one on and let him do the sucking.

But some people seem to be immune to adder bites. I once had a keeper on an Essex marsh where adders abounded. He was one of the real old-fashioned semi-web-footed, rough and ready 'yellow bellies.' Adder catching was his hobby and his beer-money. Morning after morning he went out with his old retriever Nell, with two canvas bags and a pronged stick. I have known him catch sixteen adders in a morning, simply by pinning them down with a stick and then picking them up with his bare hands and dropping them one after the other into the canvas bag. Both he and his old dog had been bitten numberless times, but it seemed to make no difference to either of them. He sold the adders to the local hospital, where their fat was boiled down to make anti-snake-bite serum.

Adders, like grass-snakes, can swim splendidly. Both of them eat any number of field mice, voles, small frogs, beetles, and other 'small deer' which are found in and about the water. They swim fast with their heads just above the water, but are quite capable of diving and carrying on beneath the surface for some distance.

Grass-snakes have one bad habit; they suck eggs. I have several times had cases reported to me of grass-snakes which have climbed up in the low bushes and robbed the nests of small birds of their eggs, and I once heard of a snake being discovered in a magpie's nest at least eighteen feet above the ground. But although I have studied snakes for years I have only once seen one actually in the process of sucking eggs. It was a grass-snake, and we found it in a hen's nest, curled round a clutch of eggs busily sucking the contents out of one. But I believe that this is a very rare occurrence.

Snakes move fast when alarmed. In grass they are able to travel quickly because by moving rapidly from side to side they exert constant leverage and propulsive movement against the stems of grass. But on open ground they 'row' themselves forward by opening and contracting the scales underneath their bodies. These scales are actually connected with the tips of the ribs, so that a snake is able to exert a very considerable amount of muscular power.

All snakes cast their skins once or twice a year. This is known as 'sloughing,' but an odd thing about the adder is that when it does so it sloughs its skin from the tip of its nose to the end of its tail and actually casts off the outer covering of its eyes in the process. This is a sort of thin membrane. Not only does it protect the snake's eyes from dust but it actually acts as a pair of spectacles, since the membrane is able to magnify to a slight degree.

Adders are different from the other two English snakes in that their young are born as complete little snakes and not hatched from eggs. There is an old and persistent legend in many country districts that when a mother adder and her young are suddenly disturbed the mother opens her mouth and the young leap straight down her throat one after the other. Many reliable naturalists and lifelong students of snakes, including old 'Brusher' Mills, the famous professional snake-catcher in the New Forest, swear that they have seen this happen. None the less, it remains unproven, for many years ago a famous sporting journal offered a prize of £10 to anyone who could produce reliable evidence, backed up by witnesses. So far the £10 has remained unpaid and unclaimed.

There is a general belief that adders are deaf, which is not so, although their vision is very limited. I think the reason why they sometimes allow themselves to be trodden on is because they lie still trusting to protective coloration.

All English snakes go into the ground, into holes and cracks, to hibernate during the winter, where they sleep for months on end, secure in an immense coat of fat. The reason why we do not see more of them during the day is because they hunt at night. They are curiously local in their habits. For example, you may year after year find a particular area of a marsh or heath, perhaps only a few acres, literally infested by adders. Yet only a mile away you may not see one from one year's end to another.

Grass-snakes grow up to four feet in length. Indeed, I once killed one nearly five feet long. They are easily tamed and soon get to know their owner.

Curiously enough, both hedgehogs and dogs have a hatred of snakes. The hedgehog, secure in his coat of bristles, kills any snake it meets, ruthlessly and mercilessly, crushing its backbone just at the back of the neck between its small, powerful teeth; while terriers frequently make a hobby of snake killing, whirling them round their heads until they seem to be encircled by a mass of reptile.

So when next you see a snake in England, unless it is an adder, spare it. It does little harm and lots of very useful vermin killing.

III

I am monarch of all I survey;
My right there is none to dispute;
From the centre all round to the sea
I am lord of the fowl and the brute.
                              WILLIAM COWPER

We are at strange work on the marshes to-day, work that reverses the art and the practice of centuries. We are turning back the pages that three hundred years of dearly bought experience of drainage have taught us. Here on the East Coast where the flat horizons of great cattle marshes, wide and lonely as prairies, are bounded only by the sea-walls, we are faced by a problem which probably occurs only once in half a century. The drought is the cause. The fleets and dykes have dried up. Where normally are broad and reed-fringed shining lagoons, the haunt of duck and waders, the home of enormous eels, to-day we find brown sun-baked areas of mud, fissured by cracks so wide that a baby moorhen can fall down them and never get out again.

The water has gone. That means a bad season for wildfowl. The same thing happened in 1933 and 1932. The home-bred duck refused to breed. And when the autumn rains fell and the fleets and dykes filled tardily it was found that their waters were rank and foul. The duck would not come to them, and the sheep and cattle which drank from them suffered scour, gripes, and sickness.

164

So this summer we are blocking up the outfall, throwing clay-banks across the drainage ditches, coaxing every drop of precious water from the upland land drains on to the bosom of the marshes, where normally water is our enemy.

It has had an odd effect, this sudden and paralysing drought. It has upset not only the plans of the farmer and the marsh grazier, but it has upset also that older and more mysterious routine, the migration of birds. For thousands of years the wild-fowl and the waders from the North have dropped in on the still dawns and quiet nights of these summer days, weary after their flights from Scandinavia and the Baltic, to feed and to breed on these quiet marshes where the red-sailed barges and the oyster-smacks drift like unearthly ships above the ramparts of the sea-walls.

On an early dawn I set sail in my gunning-punt from that old island of the Dane which most good gunners know to sail up a mile-long tidal creek to a marsh where we are nursing a decoy pond, its once broad waters now shrunken to a mere puddle.

It is only at night and in the quiet hours of dawn that the marsh gunner at this time of year may tell with certainty how little or how much of bird life is breeding on the marsh. It is then that the migrants drop in, the nesting duck are abroad and unafraid.

They come, these wanderers, in the quiet of the sleeping hours, a far, high whimper of wings, cutting the old airways.

Faint and high the voices come down—tiny whistles and

pipings, twitterings and flutings, dim bell-like notes—a strange wind-borne choir.

Greenland and the white wastes of Novaya Zemlya, the marshes of Finland, the unnamed lochs and estuaries of those far Lofoten Islands where once we caught salmon by the unearthly light of the Midnight Sun—these were the lands which last saw the birds who now drop down in my Essex marsh from the stars—whimbrel, greenshank, sanderling, garganey, and the rest.

With a rag of sail and the cold, fair wind of breaking day, the punt drifts up the creek, low and grey, almost invisible. Behind lies the island and its elms, the Saxon church, the inn which they built in the Wars of the Roses, the manor-house whose deeds were signed in Elizabeth's reign, the green and grassy Roman theatre that was all white marble and strong brick when Carausius hid his galleys in this very creek and the Count of the Saxon Shore patrolled these moonlit marshes with his legions.

The old yellow-walled farms are asleep within their moats. A far dog bays on Peldon Hill. The world of men is still asleep. But the marsh is alive. From Deadman's Point, where the Salcott smugglers slew the gaugers, to Pennyhole Fleet where the black-headed gulls nest in their thousands, the whole wide marsh is alight and alive with birds. There is no trackway on it and no man. It is green and rough with thistles, cut by dykes and shining fleets. Sleeping cattle rise like humped islands above the thin ground mist. Great reed-beds, where bittern have nested and none been the wiser, show dense and forest-like in the dawn, the brown tassels of last winter hung with shining dew.

The sharp nose of the punt slides like a great knife into the soft mud of the salting 'cant.' Even the silken ripple of our passage is silent.

I sit and wait. Slowly the tide brims in between the saltings and the sea-lavender. The shining muds go under. Rabbits stir in the bleached grass on the sea wall. Rooks flap up the tide-line. A carrion crow, forsaking that twisted grove on the Ray Island, a mile away, croaks as he drifts over the Point. When Hasting the Dane laid up his fighting ships in this long creek——this 'hoe' as we still call it in the old Danish——such a dawn-croak meant sightless eyes to any poor devil who lay wounded in the smoking ruins of thorpe or wooden hall.

Suddenly the flat grey of dim water and dimmer marshes takes on a new light. A young green grows in the east, floods up over the grey and waiting sea. The sky turns from the indigo of night to apple green. Small fleecy clouds blush pink at their edges like débutantes caught in the bath.

Reed warblers swing in the tall reeds, their reeling song suddenly inspired. A pair of duck come straight and low over my head——so low that one could hit them with a salmon rod. A very different story from the bitter days of February when they rose half a mile away at the glint of winter sun on a gun-barrel.

From a rabbit hole in the sea wall a snaky and inquisitive head, brilliant green, a crimson beak, bright and liquid eyes,

167

peers forth—a nesting sheld-duck. Oblivious of the punt and the watching man, she waddles out—pure white neck, deep rich chestnut waistcoat, white belly, the handsomest and largest duck in England. Then she is off on quick wings. The cock follows—and four more! Here is one of those communal, disused rabbit burrows in which two, three, or more of these large duck will sometimes rear their joint families in harmony.

High overhead comes a faint, clear, tittering call—seven long-legged birds, graceful as dancers, dropping on pointed wings from the green depths of the morning sky. Their clear call rings through the light marsh mist, clear as the note of those Seven Ghostly Whistlers of Ben Alder whom you may hear any day of fog on the slopes of that grand deer forest of the North. The whimbrel are here. In one swift dropping swoop they are down in the shallows of the dewy pond, dipping, running on twinkling feet, dancing in the fleet waters. They wash off the salt of Spanish marismas, the white brine of the Zuider Zee.

And all around, on looped and quivering wings, hang the redshank, their clear bell-like notes filling the marsh and the dawn. They swoop and quiver, soar and stoop, flash like arrows across the creek.

Down on the shrunken lower pools the gulls cackle and shout in their thousands. A great horde of starlings rises from the reedbeds of the decoy and goes inland like an army. The sun comes up over the flat sea, thin, marshalled spears of crimson heralding his advent, and the red roof of the decoyman's cottage glows as though caught by fire. The reefed sail of a smack, sticking up over the far sea-wall, is suddenly alight. For a brief moment it is aflame in the young sun——one, then another, till all the fishing fleet is lit and alive——on fire in a Hobbema furnace of ochre and crimson.

There comes that early morning sound of the immemorial tidal ways——the slow creak and rattle of lifting anchor chains. Slowly the sails break out and fill, the boats steal down the creek——ships sailing above the green marsh——and the fishing fleet puts out to sea and the soles which await them in the swatchways.

A heron flaps over the sea-wall on great slow wings, lifts suddenly like a blown rag as he sights the silent gun-punt, swings down-wind with a hoarse *fra-aank! fra-aank!*——a veritable echo of Norman England, and is away in a deuce of a hurry for so dignified an English gentleman.

The sun lightens and strengthens. Already the terns are dipping above the flooding tide. The punt lifts on the rising water, swings free of the mud. Cattle move and low. A bull bellows somewhere beyond the stunted willows of the decoy pond. More duck pass on purposeful wings. Up the tide-edge, a bare foot above the water, dashes a trip of oxbirds. They turn suddenly, fall like a shoal of dropping silver and are away again——the last stragglers of winter, the 'plovers' pages' of the old gunners, who swore that they waited like lackeys on the hosts of golden plover in winter. Soon they too will be on the wing——travelling thousands of feet above the sea, beyond the eye of man, on that stupendous migration journey which takes them to Spitsbergen and half around the globe.

It is time to move. The punt swings into the channel, the sprit-sail fills, she gathers way, surges down to the sea and the island of the Dane—and as, half an hour later, I tack in under that 'tempesty corner' of the chalk-faced sea-walls where three tideways meet and the open sea lies empty and vast, save for the far sails of the fishing fleet, there passes overhead a far and noble raider—a mere dot in the high skies, a peregrine on his lordly passage from Findhorn or Forth down by the narrow seas of England to the steaming marshes of Spain, the great lagoons of the Guadalquivir where the wild camels stalk.

I have seen perhaps fifty duck where I should have seen two hundred. Those that are nesting will not stay. Like the peregrine they too will fly south to Spain. And we poor gunners will once again count our daily bags on the fingers of one hand—unless the rain comes soon and in plenty.

WIDGEON

AUGUST

I

From troubles of the world
I turn to ducks.
F. W. HARVEY
Ducks and Other Verses

THROUGHOUT the summer my ducks lived gloriously. Their world was their own. In a dim, green wilderness of reeds, furrowed by snaky channels of peat-stained water, opening here and there into little lakes and bays, they made their nests, laid their creamy-coloured eggs, fed and slept happily in a silence broken only by the wind running through the reeds, the reed-warblers reeling their interminable song.

The eggs cracked, chipped, and broke, and the tiny little balls of down, with their ridiculously wide eyes, their absurdly business-like little bills, appeared.

They scuttled about the still surfaces of the fen-pools like energetic pills. The haste and agility of their movements was fantastic. It seemed incredible that such tiny scraps of life, at one moment floating motionless, should the next suddenly furrow the surface, like tiny motor-boats leaving V-shaped wakes that sent ripples among the reeds.

The pike had one or two. A sudden bulge in the water, a foamy swirl, the scattering of the ducklings like starlets against a black sky; the momentous, terrifying appearance for a second of a pointed wicked head, wide gleaming jaws, the

173

eyes of a water tiger—and one or more of the babies had gone.

They said that the heron, that lonely, grey fisher who drifted in over the reed-beds like a blown rag, gulped one or two of them as a man might gulp an oyster.

But I do not believe that. Even if it is true I will not believe it. For the heron is too splendid a relic of medieval England, too grand an ornament of the sky, to be sacrificed to the keeper's gun.

I dare say the brown rats on the water's edge killed a few. They would kill and eat their own mothers. The carrion crows picked the young ones up slyly.

And once or twice the great blue-grey Montagu harrier, that noble bird of prey who beats the fens like a setter and swings high in the sky above the reeds, the water, the gleaming dykes and lodes, above the peat diggings and the tousled-headed willows—he certainly took his toll. He picked them off the water with a sudden graceful swoop, taking their tiny lives as unconsidered trifles.

But I allow him that. For there are not many Montagu harriers in England, and the sight and memory of the pair of them, noble in their air-borne beauty, is something to wake the shadows of Elizabethan England.

These are the perils they endured, the enemies they suffered. We cared for them and protected them, the seventy-year-old-wise Fen keeper and I, as best we might. For, after all, it is only a year ago that we decided that this two hundred acres of wet, sour land, growing reeds, and coarse litter-grass, scorned by cattle and dangerous for horses, could be put to better and more primitive values if we forsook the unequal battle between bog and water, and let the water take possession once more.

The result to-day is a piece of the old primeval fen, the fens that sheltered Hereward the Wake against the Conqueror, reborn in the heart of those beleaguering marshes of the Isle of Ely where the Last of the English made his stand.

Two years ago a duck was a rarity. To-day the fen is full of them. The Montagu harrier patrols the wide skies, a destroyer of the upper air. The reed-warblers swing and chatter in the reeds like feathered mice.

Duck of every sort bibble and spatter, dive and quack.

The brown peaty waters have spread again where once the Saxon waded on his stilts. The place has recovered its spirit, its ancient soul.

So all through the spring and the summer the duck nested and reared their young. Then one day I saw sixteen or twenty pair suddenly marshal their young in agitated flotillas, rise from the water in a scuttering rush and swing high, ever higher, in widening circles above the fens.

The young ducks, past their first hesitancy on the wing, followed boldly. From the reeds in the water five hundred of them swung in tremendous arcs, fretted against the blue of the rain-washed sky.

It was like a huntsman casting off his hounds—the captain of a ship in new waters sounding his way in order to gain some authentic knowledge of the fairway that would decide his future courses.

These young ducks were trying out the tides and currents of the upper air. Fresh from the safety of those small, flower-decked pools, safe in the green mystery of the reed beds, they were now on wing, five hundred feet above the flat levels of Cambridgeshire.

By some strange, ten-thousand-year-old inherited instinct, unexplained as yet by the slick scientific philosophies of to-day, they were scenting the air, testing the tidal currents of the wind, sensing their direction.

With brains weighing scarcely a quarter of an ounce, these not yet fully-fledged birds were contemplating a sudden, momentous journey to the landes of Southern France, the marismas of Spain, the broad and swollen lagoons of the Guadalquivir, where the last wild camels in Europe, echoes of the Morisco wars—now by a tragic irony refought once again—roam in hump-backed, solitary grotesqueness, over lands that have known neither the plough nor the spade of the husbandman since history began.

After two or three such initial flights there came a morning when suddenly the whole combined squadrons of the shovellers rose into the air as one, and, as under the leadership of one supreme air marshal, turned their beaks south by south-east and set off in a steady purposeful flight. They flew high above Cambridge, high over Saffron Walden, high over the River of London, probably passing Dover, flood-lit in the garish showmanship of our present time.

And so south by south-east over the tumbled, troubled water of Biscay, above the wastes of the landes, above the gunfire of the Spanish civil wars, the murders, the shooting, and the bitterness.

The bombers and the fighters roar beneath them. The propagandist broadcasts serrate the ether. The air is full of the voice and the menaces of a new civilization. Mankind has taken to the airways of the birds in order to destroy the beauty, the loveliness, the humanity, and the grace of which the birds themselves typify a part.

Above it all, through the mess and the muck, above the noise, destruction, and the bloodshed, the duck that were bred in the green stillness of my Cambridgeshire fen fly southward to the land of the Moor.

II

Now, with her challenging grouse, and her sea-silver salmon,
August, of mountains and memories, comes to her own;
Would you gaze into the crystal, and see the long valleys,
Braes of the North, and the rivers that wander between,
Crags with whose coating the tint of the ptarmigan tallies?

PATRICK CHALMERS
Green Days and Blue Days

Before you lies the brown and purple upward sweep of the moor. To the right, the dazzling waters of the Minch, a wrinkled sea-floor of crawling waves, set with the little isles that lie like polished stones in the beaten silver of the west. And behind you, crouched on the peaty floor of the butt, a loader and a retriever.

From somewhere far ahead over the rim of the moor, where the heather meets the sky, comes, faint and far, a whistle. Another, and another. The retriever stiffens. The loader becomes electric. The vision of bee-lazy moorland crystallizes in a split second into a tense focusing on that rim of sky immediately in front.

You heed neither the raven's croak from the high hill on the leftward march nor the mewing of the buzzards who swing in half-mile circles. The whaup's whistle has lost its lonely music.

Suddenly, away on the right flank, a red flag bobs above the heather. Another whistle—and another. And, in an instant, sixteen hurtling black cannon-balls shoot over the moorland rim like cricket balls and hurl themselves at your head. The gun jumps to the shoulder—*bang!*—a stinging crack, the acrid smell of burnt powder—*bang!*—a yard in front this time, and, hit full and square in the head, the old cock crumples like a burst shell in the heather, a floating plume of feathers his funeral shroud.

And then they are up and over you—a mile-a-minute—with a mere fraction of a second in which to think and act. You half turn, hand the empty gun to the loader, snatch the second, ready loaded, swing round, and are on them again ere they are out of range.

If July in London has not left you slack of limb and eye you will put another in the bag, perhaps a brace. But it takes a good man, the man who shoots like a book, to kill two in front and two behind.

So, when people talk about the slaughter of innocent grouse, when ignorant newspapers of Socialist tendencies print the words " Massacre on the moors," reflect for a moment that the driven grouse flies at a mile-a-minute, that he is on you and over like an arrow from a bow, that the average range of a game gun is only forty-five yards, that the ' killing circle ' of its charge of shot is only thirty inches at that range, and that to kill your bird you must swing and shoot with such nice judgment as to place that killing circle all round him while he is travelling at one mile a minute. It is not so easy after all.

Let me premise, for the reader who does not shoot, that the

act of driving grouse is to bring the birds forward and over the guns, who are hidden in a line of turf and heather butts, horseshoe in shape, across the particular beat of the moor which is being driven.

The beaters themselves walk slowly forward flushing the birds towards the guns. And by the time the grouse coveys reach the butt they are going full throttle.

The old method was to walk them up. This meant that one often walked almost on top of them. Whereupon the grouse got up and was duly saluted in its posterior. Somehow I cannot regard this as such an admirable form of sport as giving him more than a fair chance at a mile-a-minute when he is well up and alive to danger.

But driving as a system is not very old. It was first practised at Cannon Hall, near Barnsley in Yorkshire, and was brought to a fine art by the late General John Hall, of Six Mile Bottom and High Force, and by the sixth Lord Wal-

singham, the famous Tom de Grey, the finest game shot that ever lived.

Lord Walsingham always maintained that if a man could kill three out of five of the birds he shot at, under all and any conditions, he could safely call himself a good shot. Put thus, it does not sound difficult. But try it and see.

Lord Walsingham used to tell a story of a man who, standing in a butt which faced up a hillside down which the grouse were flying, fired at the leading bird of an oncoming pack. The bird was forty yards off and the hillside was behind it. It fell dead. At the same instant a hare leapt from the heather behind it and dropped, also dead. When they went out to pick up the hare they found it lying on one side of a clump of heather. On the other side a reddish-brown bush-tail twitched. They pulled it out—a fox, struck through the head. That surely must be a record—a grouse, a hare, and a fox at one shot. And the man who fired it had not the faintest idea that either the hare or the fox were there.

Talking of hares reminds me of the story told by my old friend, the late Lieutenant-Colonel Cyril Foley, the famous Eton, Cambridge, and Middlesex cricketer. Many years ago the ex-Kaiser and his suite were staying with King Edward VII. Shooting was provided. But the Germans, accustomed apparently to military manœuvres of the extended order variety, insisted on firing not from the shoulder, but from the hip. And when two or three hares appeared on the scene the stimulus was too great for them. Breaking from the line of guns, Wilhelm's suite charged wildly after the fleeing

animals, firing furiously from the hip and shouting " *Harsen!*
Harsen! "

No human being was actually killed during the day, but
King Edward, like Sir Clive Wigram, received a pellet in
the nose before lunch. A diplomat to the last, he merely remarked blandly, " Very dangerous! Very dangerous! " shook
his head, and wiped the blood away with his handkerchief.

After lunch, however, things improved. One German shot
another. Smack in the gaiters the victim received the charge.
He leapt a yard in the air, rubbed his leg, twirled his moustaches, and, gazing sorrowfully at his assailant, remarked in
mournful tones, " *Ach!* Do not do zat! " We must assume
that he had been shot before, but never at quite such close
range.

The day ended well. On the way home a pheasant got up.
When it was at least a hundred yards off, far beyond the range
of any shot-gun, one of the Germans unlimbered his piece,
fired, and killed it. Such a spectacular performance evoked
universal admiration. Every one wished to see the gun which
had performed this phenomenal feat. They examined it. It
was a rifle—with a killing range of a quarter of a mile!

For the whole of that day the unsuspecting countryside
round about had been subjected to undistributed, high-angle
rifle-fire. I ought to add that both the ex-Kaiser and the
Crown Prince are excellent shots and not addicted to these
unorthodox practices.

The late Ward Hunt, one of the best shots of his day, was
perhaps a little unorthodox also. Once, when shooting as a

schoolboy with the late Colonel Custance, of Weston, two pheasants got up in front of his host. Colonel Custance threw his hat into the air to make the birds rise to a good height. The fourteen-year-old Hunt promptly put two barrels through the hat and then, seizing his second gun from his loader, killed a pheasant! They do not breed good shots like that nowadays.

I am reminded that it is only a few years since the Duke of Connaught narrowly escaped being shot, at Balmoral. The charge missed him, but a single pellet struck Sir Clive (now Lord) Wigram in the nose. This fact has not before been printed. Perhaps I had better not give the name of the very distinguished person who fired the shot. He has heard enough about it already. King George V, who was present, at once ordered the offender to go home, and his bags were packed that night.

I suppose King George V, Lord Huntingfield, the late Marquess of Ripon, the late Captain Freddie Fryer, who lingers lovingly in my early memories as a donor of half-sovereigns, Sir Harry Stonor, the late Lord Downe, Corney Wykeham-Martin of Leeds Castle in Kent, and the late Lord Westbury were, with one or two others, not only the finest shots of their age and generation, but probably the best of all time. Sir Harry Stonor alone remains.

Somehow, I do not think the guns of the present day can, or will ever, equal those giants. How often do you see a man, standing under the hedges of Dullingham or Chevely, on those gorgeous September mornings when Newmarket lies half-hid beneath the mists, like a lost city of the plain, when the coveys come thick and fast like cannon-balls—how often do you see a man take two in front and two behind with that effortless ease which the late Archibald Stuart-Wortley immortalized for all time?

Who are the great ones of to-day? A few winters ago I saw the late Sir Henry Birkin have five driven coots dead in the air, using three guns from a wildfowl punt pitching in a north-east wind and a snowstorm. That was during the annual Hickling Broad coot shoot. I put it down as the finest performance I have ever seen.

They tell me that Mr Ivan Cobbold is a good shot and fires thirty thousand cartridges in a season. Mr Frank Barker is somewhere near the top of that tree on which the de Greys and the Vannecks sat for so long. Mr J. F. Mason, of Eynsham, has killed wood pigeons by the cartload. Lord Dunglass, among the younger ones, is good. And there are a few more. But not many. And none of these present ones compare in actuality with the old school. Only last season I saw my right-hand neighbour, Lord Loch of the flowing white moustaches, wipe the eyes of three bright young men in successive drives.

Are the young shots too careless—careless of their health and careless of practice? Do they smoke too much, drink too much, stay up too late, or take too little exercise? If there is a fault I should say that it is lack of practice and too little exercise.

The seat of a motor-car is not such good medicine for the

inside of a man as the outside of a horse. Who to-day walks down Piccadilly every day in July, swinging an iron walking stick weighing seven pounds? Rimington-Wilson did that every summer for forty years. He said it made his arms flexed and ready for a gun in August. And there, indeed, was one of the greatest shots that ever lived.

So our glories decline. The sport of our fathers, the art of Peter Hawker, the 'unerring tube' of Osbaldeston, has become to-day an excuse for brokers to entertain their clients, a slippery step in the ladder by which those whose blood has been ennobled by cheque-book climb their petty Olympus.

I think the best commentary on the present swing of the pendulum was provided some years ago, in 1928, I think, just before the American slump, when a grouse fell on Hunthill Moor in Aberdeenshire on August 12th. It was worth a thousand pounds. A cheque for that amount was signed and given at lunch to the man who shot it.

This plutocratic bird was the subject of a sweep among a group of Americans. The first grouse of the season was subscribed for to the tune of £1000 in what were, then, quite good dollars. These gilt-edged sportsmen had rented a castle, a moor, servants, wine, ghillies, motor-cars, beaters, and the rest of the gallery at an 'all-in' price.

What a contrast between such a party, oozing ostentatious wealth at every button-hole, gorgeous in checks, resplendent in cigars, terrific in weapons, paying an average of a pound to every bird they kill, and the sport of our forefathers!

In the old days—and not so very old either—you could go

to the Highlands and rent as much moor as you could see from a high hill for a ten-pound note. That was in the days of Colonel Thornton and Squire Osbaldeston, when our grandfathers wore top-hats to shoot in and thigh gaiters buttoned with a million buttons. They carried guns five feet long and ate bread and cheese and pickled onions for their lunch.

But they betted as high as any American of to-day. The 'Squire,' for example, once backed himself to kill a thousand partridges in two days for a wager of £1000. He challenged Lord Charles Kennedy, and, although the amount was ultimately reduced, the bet was won. But the most incredible of all the shooting eccentricities of yesterday or to-day was a magnificent personage who flourished just over a century ago.

Picture a fiery-faced gentleman, in a cutaway, green, brass-buttoned shooting coat; curly brimmed, bell-topped hat; thigh gaiters buttoned with innumerable buttons armed with a gun five feet long, astride a bull on a Yorkshire grouse moor. Ahead of this terrific Nimrod stalks a large black sow. Suddenly the sow stiffens in the heather. Its snout and head straighten out like a poker. The pig stands rigid. The bull and its rider draw nearer.

On the instant, from the heather bursts a covey of grouse like a bomb-shell. The sportsman raises his ferocious piece, an instant's deliberate aim, and the gun vomits a yard of flame and a bellying cloud of smoke. A grouse drops to the shot.

This is no Bertram Mills nightmare. It is a fact. It happened, to be accurate, about a hundred and twelve years ago. The rider of the bull was the eccentric Mr James Hirst, of Rawcliffe. He had trained the pig to point grouse as accurately as any dog. And he went hunting on the bull. The habit arose from his strenuous objection to paying taxes. Horses and dogs in those days were heavily taxed. Bulls and pigs were not. Hence the odd, but frequent, sight of a gentleman in ratcatcher attending meets of the Badsworth Hounds on a bull and shooting grouse over a pig.

Mr Hirst was not the only man to train a pig to point at game. About a hundred years ago Mr Richard Toomer, who lived in the New Forest, had a black sow which stood well to pheasants, partridges, blackgame, snipe, and rabbits. But it would not come to hare. This extraordinary animal was bought by Sir H. St John Mildmay.

For some odd reason the major field sports—shooting, hunting, and racing, the latter more properly a pastime— have always provoked extravagances of performance and betting. For example, in the same year in which Mr Hirst went shooting on his bull, Lord Kennedy took a bet of forty-to-one in fifty-pound notes that he would kill forty brace of grouse on Felar Moor in Aberdeenshire and afterwards ride to Dunnottar and back, a hundred and twenty miles, between midnight and midnight. He started shooting at 2 A.M., killed his forty brace by 8.41, changed his clothes, mounted his horse, and rode the sixty miles to Dunnottar by 2 o'clock in the afternoon. He rested an hour and started back over appallingly rocky, badly-made hill roads, crossing wild moorlands and climbing mountain-sides. He reached home by 6.47 P.M., winning his bet with four hours and three minutes in hand.

About the same time the Lord Middleton of the day commonly went partridge shooting on a bull.

But if they had some odd sportsmen in those days we have odder still to-day. But their oddities are unintentional rather than deliberate. The City squire is funny without knowing it. And the grouse shooter who gravitates from Throgmorton Street, gorgeous in checks, effulgent in cigars, resplendent in gaiters, prolific in weapons, is not only funny but tragic. The result is that some odd things happen. The grouse alone do not go in deadly peril.

III

And in the morning weather
  Your care shall spread them wings,
Lost in the seas of heather,
  Whelmed in the wind that sings;
For all that's mean or tragic,
  For all sublunar ills,
Shall melt beneath the magic
  Clean vintage of the hills.

PATRICK CHALMERS
Green Days and Blue Days

We rode up the sea road from the bay, through aisles of still, reddened pine trunks, on two cobby hill ponies, bigger than most ponies but not yet of the dignity of a horse. The laird had bought them, just a score from Uist, twenty years before, and has bred from them ever since. They will carry a man almost anywhere that a goat can climb. Their hoofs were studded with nails an eighth of an inch square.

We turned off the roads and into a glen, broad and noble, stretching into the blue and savage solitudes of the hills. On the right of the track, the mere shadow of a path across the rabbit-nibbled turf, a salmon river slid and chattered to the sea. Two hundred yards across the turf we turned our ponies into the river, forded it with solemn, catlike steps, each hoof kicking up a thin veil of golden-brown water. On the far bank the track wound on and upwards, climbing all the time.

The hills grew nearer to meet us on the other side. Their

189

faces became bolder, more aridly barren. Red sandstone and bluish-grey granite thrust itself in peaks and massive shoulders against the hot blue of an August sky. Ahead, the mountains loomed steep and terrific.

In this part of Scotland, north of Loch Maree, there is scenery to rival any in the world. Small wonder that the shepherds and stalkers bred in these steep glens, beneath these stark hills, have gone out with their sheepdogs and their long hill sticks to Patagonia and Chile, to Peru and Bolivia, the first shepherds in the world to conquer the Andes on foot and with their dogs. John Cameron of Strath na Shellaig was indeed the first man to cross the Andes with his dogs. With him we were to spend the night. It was to his bothy that we rode into the hills on a narrow stony track that rose higher each mile above the brawling Gruinard river.

As we rode in the hot stillness of that afternoon, the creak of saddle leather and the clink of stones the only sound, there dawned suddenly upon me the incredible realization that this glen, these lonely hills, this tumbling, urgent river had not changed a tittle or lost the slightest shadow of their dignity since Doctor Johnson was suddenly smitten into comparative silence by the beauty of the Highlands more than a century ago. Queen Victoria wrote her dutiful and domestic *Pages from a Highland Diary*, inspired by just such scenery to a temporary forgetfulness of the priggishness of Gladstone, the fawnings of Disraeli, the pomposities of Palmerston.

Have you ever reflected upon the peculiar, lifeless silence of a deer forest? There is practically no bird life and few animals. There are none of the pleasant, domestic, almost farmyard incidences of such homely English creatures as pheasants and partridges, let alone blackbirds, thrushes, pigeons, or even sparrows. The impudence of the robin and the creeping confidences of the wren are repelled by the silence and the stones.

Here and there, in the bracken on the river flats, a few rabbits scuttled apologetically. On the river shallows the water ouzels flicked their tails and dived like otters. They can swim under water at an incredible speed, using both their wings and their legs as fins. There is no myth about this. It is a fact.

At a bend in the river, where a hundred yards of water slid smooth and still over a deep stretch of mud and waving weeds, six great white and noble birds, half the size of geese, dived and swam. As our ponies came suddenly into view, silhouetted against the sky a hundred and fifty feet above them, they swam suddenly together, a panic cluster, and then on quick, sharp-cutting wings, rose and flashed round the bend, up the river. Goosanders, the fishers of the salmon river, the spirit duck of the north. They are as wild and wary as eagles, as skilled divers as cormorants, as wide in their range over the Arctic world as the brent goose.

Then we dipped into a wide strath, green and pleasant. A burn chattered across its bosom to join the river. Clumps of bracken stood brown against the emerald of grass and the blue and purple of scattered fingers of heather. The over-thrown banks and skeleton stone walls of a deserted croft, century-old relics of the Highland clearances scarred the strath like the faint letterings of a faded manuscript. A score of Highland cattle, immense, shaggy coated, golden brown, their broad heads surmounted by the yard-wide sweep of tremendous horns, gazed at us with soft eyes that belied the seeming ferocity of their presence.

Like the sheep and the wild goats, like the deer and the wild cat, they are out on the hills all the year round, in sun and snow, in rain and frost, the survival of the fittest. Their feeding and their mating, their living and their loving are undirected by man. These are the true creatures of the forest with the eagles and the ravens, the goosanders and the ouzels.

On the hillside to the right, a straggling wood of ancient birches clung like twisted witches to a rocky scarp. It went up almost as sheer as the wall of a house. The top of one tree mingled with the roots of the trees above.

Here was the wood of the wild cats, the home of the raven, the rocks above it the haunt of the peregrines.

As our little procession of two wound upward, riding solemnly into the hills like a Boer commando, there came quietly on the still air, a queer, semi-subdued, yet quite distinct *clink! clink!* It was almost a metallic note, yet obviously the voice of a bird. We reined in. Listened. There it came again. *Clink! clink!* It puzzled us both. There was a clear note of warning in that lost, double monosyllable of the hill solitude.

The stalker was not sure what it was. He knew nothing

" A great bird sailed out over the glen."

about birds. Few of them do. He thought it was a snipe—
or a golden plover. Or even a raven. But it lacked that
deeper, more sinister, almost mocking note of the raven's
hollow clank.

Clink! clink! From the topmost green of the old birch-
trees, from a rock a thousand feet sheer against the skyline, a
great bird sailed out over the glen, high above the river, its
wings spread wider than the height of a tall man, the great
feathers of its wing-tips sharp cut against the sky like out-
spread fingers. Two slow flaps and it glided a hundred yards.
Two more flaps and it slid through the hot air a quarter mile.
An effortless wing-beat or two and it banked upward,
wheeled round the shoulder of a mountain-top and faded
into the distance towards Fannich. A golden eagle.

We saw two more on the way up to the loch. Once a pair
of buzzards mewed above us in half-mile circles. Then the
loch came in sight, five miles long, nearly a mile wide, wind-
ing into the dark hills like a twisted shield of silver. We left
the ponies at the loch head, their forelegs hobbled, to graze
at will and wait the coming of the ghillie who would take
them back.

The boat, broad and beamy, was launched over the stones
with a sudden chattering rattle. It took the water with a
swish. The stalker pointed silently upward. There on a bluff
above the river, where loch and river met, silhouetted against
the evening sky stood a wild goat. His horns were curled
and magnificent. His head and outline were massive and
ancient. He stood there, epitome of the ancient world, as his

forebears had stood on the hills in Palestine above Galilee two thousand years before—the ancient, slit-eyed, pondering goat, half-emblem of the devil, a queer almost satanic spirit of the hills, looking down upon these disturbers of the mountain peace that had been his since the dawn of time.

Even so the Rocky Mountain sheep watched the coming of the pioneers of the Far West. The mouflon of Northern Africa stood in the same impassive manner on just such barren hills and watched the caravans of the Queen of Sheba wind southward into the desert. He stood there like a monument cut in stone, unmoving. And presently, on a lower ledge, sharp-cut against the sky, turning now to apple-green, four other heads, horned, bearded, and inquisitive, poked themselves over the skyline. Three nannygoats and a kid, three-quarters grown. They stood there immovable, dutifully a ledge below their master.

The boat moved on up the loch, the long oars cutting silkily into the water, the cormorants watching from the rocks like hideous parsons, the shadows dropping down from the hills, the five goat heads cut out in a devilish fresco against the fading light of the Atlantic west.

High on the hill, five hundred feet above the face of the black rocks that stepped sheer down into the black waters like prison walls, a thin high scream sounded suddenly, was cut short. A hideous yowl like a demon's laughter, echoed across the loch. The oars dipped and fell.

" The cats will be on the walk," the stalker remarked. The smoke of his pipe curled blue in the suddenly chilled air.

A mile away, from a dark corrie that gashed the opposite hills, there came a deep, menacing *clonk! clonk!* It had the sound of blood in it, a mocking note of death. The raven was answering the wild cat. The oars creaked, a salmon swirled on the shallows. Somewhere a big sea trout plopped noisily. Ahead, a faint yellow pin-point of light gleamed in the single window of the stalker's bothy above the yellow beach. Night slipped, cold and immense, from the mountainsides. An everyday, uneventful Highland day had ended.

195

IV

ALWAYS GRACEFUL, a roebuck is particularly so when stripping
some young tree of its leaves, nibbling them off one by one in the
most delicate and dainty manner. I have watched a roe strip the
leaves of a long bramble, beginning at one end and nibbling off
every leaf. My rifle was aimed at its heart and my finger was on
the trigger, but I made some excuse or other to myself for not
killing him, and left him undisturbed—his beauty saved him.

CHARLES ST JOHN
Wild Sports and Natural History of the Highlands

A year ago this month, under a full harvest moon, I was
taken out on a Scottish hillside by a friend to hunt the most
alert animal in Britain. We went with rifles, under a full and
golden moon, through an old wood of wind-bent birches and
tall pines, their rough trunks reddened by the autumn suns
of a hundred years. We trod quietly, like Indians.

The valley lay below us, a vast trough, full of a sea of
grey mist, a sheep's wool floor that eddied.

It was very still and quiet, rather damp, with a touch of
frost—and the moon was a still and golden glory. It was a
world such as you who walk by day only can never know.

We waited, on that silent, owl-haunted hillside, a quarter-
mile apart. Each stood behind the trunk of a great pine.
We stood tense and listening.

The quiet of the night was eloquent about us. On such a
night Fingal, the hound of Ossian, walked the hill in search
of the wild red deer.

196

But on this particular night, as I stood behind an ancient pine in Argyllshire, I expected no red deer, had no hound of Ossian crouching at my feet. I waited for the roe.

If you were to ask any good naturalist which animal was the quickest and sharpest in all Britain he might easily say the roe.

The red deer is dead in Dorset and Hampshire. He is a faint memory in Sussex. I have never heard of one in Wiltshire. He is not a native of the Welsh marches. When they drive those high coverts of the Timberline, the animal that most often breaks forth is not a red stag—that would be history—nor a fallow buck, for he would be a mere park escape—but the roe.

The red stag lives to-day in Devon and Somerset, solely because he is protected. If he were not protected in order that he might be hunted he would not endure a month. He would be shot, trapped, snared, and hunted out of existence. But the red deer is spared these indignities. He is regarded as a beast of noble chase. Every excuse is made for him. Unwritten laws are written about him. You cannot do this and you cannot do that. But the roe, to many people and to most keepers, is sheer vermin. Yet the roe survives in these counties of Dorset, Wiltshire, Hampshire, Sussex, and other parts of England where the red deer has long been extinct. Why?

Stand with me for a moment behind that old red pine trunk on an Argyll hillside, on a night of moon and mist and silence, and you will know the answer.

197

It was quite quiet. The owls hooted, dimly in the old wood, like Icelandic echoes. Far below, on the shingly beach of the sea-loch, the sea crawled silkily. Its little waves came and went on the small stones of the beach. A diver, somewhere far up the loch, laughed crazily, a sudden lunatic sound. It was the laugh of a loon, the maniac voice that is a universal part of all mountain and forest solitudes where there is water in the hollows. The grebes and the divers are as much a part of the Canadian backwoods as they are of the long Scottish sea-lochs that creep like silver fingers into the black folds of the hills.

And then suddenly, even as that laughter echoed across the Sound of Mull, down the aisle of the pines in front of me came the roe. He was a buck, followed by a doe, both treading delicately. They moved without a sound, slight and graceful figures in the moonlight.

They came, the pair of them, like figures in a dream. And even as I debated, smitten in that sudden second, whether to shoot or not, they were gone. It may have been the moon on the rifle barrel, the rustle of sleeves as I raised my arm or just, and more probably, the mere *sense* of movement—but where there had been roe there was no longer any living thing. Merely a crackling of twigs, a sudden sideways bound, a quick thumping among the silent pines—and again the Argyllshire hillside was empty of all but the owls and the moon.

Now consider the roe. It stands not much higher than the waist of a man. It weighs on the average no more than fifty pounds. A normal head is only six points. Compare it to a red stag and it is a Pekingese beside an Alsatian. But it has twice the brains, twice the wits, twice the senses and faculties of the red deer. Perhaps that is because it is monogamous. The red stag is brutally polygamous. But the roe has only one wife and sticks to her.

And all records show that monogamous animals have just about double the intelligence of the light lovers. Which is why the roe survives.

No animal is better camouflaged by Nature. A roe doe can stand facing you against a bank of bracken in broad day-light at fifty yards, quite motionless, and you will not see her. At night you will not hear her—except perhaps for the sudden crack of a twig, or a short low sigh—or perhaps that quick, snake-like hiss which is a refinement of Nature's protection. More than one four-footed animal gets away from danger by imitating, however unconsciously, the hiss of a snake.

In the old days there were men in the South of England, and others in the Highlands of Scotland, who made the hunting of roe a fine art. They were creatures of the night, true Deerfoots, the Leatherstockings of our woods. They matched cunning with cunning, quiet with quiet. They were out under the moon, alone with the owls, waiting for the roe. They did not, and the few survivors do not, rely on beaters, butts, hounds, or broad daylight. Theirs was an equal battle of wits. And usually the roe won.

I have known a man sit in a tree to shoot a roe, merely

because he studied the air currents. Knee-high the air was still and motionless. There the little mists rose waveringly, like the smoke of small candles lit in the bracken. But about one's waist a light breeze stirred. The wind was damp and moving. And at that height the roe would smell one. So he climbed into the tops of pollard willows, into old and stunted oaks, into the bushy fastnesses of bent birch trees— and took the chance of a shot at a roe, as it stood, a brief ghost in the moon, sniffing the traitorous wind.

SEPTEMBER

I

Now shall our *Hawkes* and we be blythe, Dame *Partridge*
    ware your pate :
Our murdring *Kites*, in all their *flights*, will sild or never
    never never seld or never misse,
To trusse you ever ever ever ever, and make your bale our
    blisse.

      .   .   .   .   .

This was a fayre and a *Kingly flight*,
We *Falkners* thus make *sullen Kites* yeeld pleasure fit
    for Kings,
And sport with them in those delights, and oft, and oft in
    other things, and oft in other things.

                        THOMAS RAVENSCROFT
                      Hawking for the Partridge, 1614

PICTURE a prince, a prince on a horse, a prince in a turban and a white burnous, with the nose of an eagle, the air of an emperor, a hawk on his fist, and all the sea winds of Kent in his blowing robes.

And having pictured this to yourself see the prince as the central figure of a frieze of falconers with hawks on fist, set against the green scarp of a sheep down, the flat green floor of the marshes at their feet, the beaten silver of the sea flung beyond to the farther rim of the sky.

This pretty play of medievalism you may see on the high downs of the ancient Isle of Sheppey, where the sheep graze above the sea-ways of those nobler reaches of the Thames which are more North Sea than London River. Here, on the isle where the Roman rode out to cast his hawk at the wild-fowl of the saltings, where, they say, the Roman still walks under the moon, we, who are the last devotees of that ancient and noble sport, are met for a flight at the partridges of the sheep-walks.

There are not above fifty members of the British Falconers' Club. Fifty men to practise the sport of princes, the sport which set a noble above a commoner, whose very nomenclature divided men more rigorously into ranks than any newly minted peeress of the contracting classes.

Nineteen centuries ago when Christ walked in Galilee men rode out in the shrill Syrian dawn to hawk the buck of the plains, the gazelle of the hills. Nine hundred years ago William's Norman lords threw their hawks at the heronshaw and mallard on these same sea fringes of Kent.

And to-day when men still hold lands of the King by

PINTAIL DUCKS

serjeantry of hawks which they never pay, falconry has declined until it is the sport of a handful, an antique play, a diversion for men with Oxford minds.

Yet it is a sport demanding the utmost thought and care, the most meticulous personal attention. You cannot buy a hawk ready made. You must make and train it yourself in long hours of patience, sitting up with it far into the night until it falls asleep on your fist. When that happens you may know that the wildest bird in Britain has acknowledged you as its master. And within six weeks of the merlin, peregrine, or goshawk being taken from its nest on the moors of York-shire or in the forests of Germany it will fly to your fist, feed from hand, answer your call.

And when, as on this still and golden harvest morning, you stand on the hump-backed vallum of a British earth-work, all the sea and the marshes at your feet, the wind in your face, the hawk on your fist, you may know that you are, for a brief space, an heir of the ages. A minor page of history has turned back a thousand years.

The line of falconers advances, men and boys, some with the lordly goshawk on fist—the great hawk which can strike down a hare or bind to a heron—some with peregrines, the partridge-hawk; some with the fussy, fireworky sparrow-hawk; others with that delicate, gallant little fighting machine, the merlin, the lady's hawk. And away on the right flank, cantering on a white horse, like a figure from a tapestry, in robes and turban, the man who has helped to make British falconry a new and nascent thing, Nawab Malik

Sir Umar Hayat Khan, Chief of Tiwana, president of this club which has revived the sport of old, dead kings.

And now you will see a different flight. From somewhere far out on the flats of Foulness a rook beats heavily in from sea, high above the saltings and the sheep walks, a dot in the sky. Charles Knight, that prince of falconers, unhoods his tiercel, raises his fist high and forward in the direction of that high voyager of the sky. The falcon's eyes pick up the rook in a second—a sudden upward throw, a lightning flick of wings, an ascending sweep in one effortless curve, and almost in a breath of time the falcon is high above the rook, five hundred feet from earth.

He twists, a sudden sickening stoop to earth, wings half shut, a breath-taking dive, downward at eighty miles an hour—he is on the rook. You expect to see a whirl of feathers, a mid-air duel of sudden death . . . and instead the falcon shoots past the rook, down, down, down . . . flattens out, sweeps up again, mounts high above the quarry, who, having in one lightning twist saved his bacon, is now going flat out for Dover, France, and Eastern Europe, and stoops again at lightning speed. A floating whorl of feathers in mid-air, a struggling mass a hundred and fifty yards up, and falcon and quarry inextricably come to earth half a mile away.

That is where the horses come in.

But not all falconry is so seemingly easy, not all falcons so well trained. There are hawks which sulk when they have stooped and missed; hawks which sit in trees for hours and make fools of their masters; hawks which wet their wings in the dew and refuse to fly at all; hawks which traitorously, understandably, mount higher and higher, fade from sight and sleep that night not upon the blocks in the mews but upon some far, forgotten cliff ledge, a thousand feet above the crawling sea, the wrinkled waves.

But there are not many such renegades. It is an odd fact that a hawk, wildest and fiercest of birds, takes readily to man, tames comparatively easily, while a sparrow dies almost inevitably in captivity.

You may pay what you will for a hawk, from a shilling to the bumpkin who climbs a tree and brings a sparrow-hawk from the nest, to the two or three pounds which is the price of a noble gos from the forests of Germany. But when once you have got him the rest remains with yourself. You cannot train a hawk by deputy or machine. You cannot follow him in a motor-car. You cannot set a clock to mark the limit of his flight or prophesy by rote the miles he will lead you.

You can, in fact, set no modern standards to govern this most ancient of all sports. But if you have a little, a very little money, an infinity of patience, and a chord of history in your heart, you may practise it and become an heir of all the ages. Which is why there are only half a hundred of us.

Avebury, lost village of Ancient British earthworks, is the spiritual home of falconry in England to-day. There, not long ago, I stood on the green mound of a forgotten king, with a dozen hawks on fist about me, and saw the rolling downs of Wiltshire flow beneath our feet.

There were twelve of us, ten active falconers and two lookers on. Of that ten, nine were members of the family that has probably done more to keep alive the spirit of falconry in this country at the present day. Captain C. W. R. Knight and his brother, Mr Hugh D. Knight, who is honorary secretary of the British Falconers' Club, have done a great work between them; the first by educating the general public, through his lectures and films, to an appreciation of the beauty of a falcon on wing, and the second by his unremitting work for the Club. Perhaps the best testimony to their joint work is the fact that half of the present members of the Club are in their twenties, or younger.

The Club holds no official hawking meetings, but its members gather from time to time at certain spots throughout England, where one may still find that desirable but uncommon combination of open country, few or no trees and a reasonable supply of rooks and small game. It is probably wise not to advertise these meetings, for in these days of humanitarian busybodies even the most ancient of sport is liable to be made the target for ill-judged and ignorant attack.

But Avebury has a hawking tradition all its own. For close on a hundred years its tiny street of thatched cottages, its ancient Red Lion Inn and its huge sheltering elms, nestling within the centre of that huge ring of outer earthworks which saw the dawn of Britain, has seen each summer a gathering of falconers with hawks on fist.

And to-day, the sporting tradition of its farmers is maintained by the descendants of those who farmed these lands a century ago. Through their generosity, this sport of old, dead kings has been given a welcome for years on the hills and downs that knew the same scenes five hundred years ago.

Hawking is a game of infinite patience—patience in training your bird, patience in waiting for him to come out of a tree when he has decided to sit and stare, patience when your hawk disappears for ever, and patience again when you must take and train a new successor.

One of the questions which Mr Hugh Knight is most often asked is where one may buy trained hawks. The answer is that there are none. No falconer sells his bird except in exceptional circumstances. But the supply of birds from the nest is still sufficient to satisfy the modest need of the few falconers of to-day. There are one or two estates in this country, one of which is a large property belonging to a member of the Club, where the keepers are instructed to watch and preserve all broods of hawks.

The period of training varies according to the skill and patience of the trainer and the aptitude of the pupil.

Most of the falcons and hawks out in September are not more than six weeks old. To the outsider the feat of training so wild a bird as a tiercel or merlin to fly from the fist, stoop at a thrown lure and return to its owner in so short a space of time is nothing short of marvellous. And after all, half the fun of falconry is in watching your bird come to the lure —a bunch of feathers that is whirled above your head on a twelve-foot length of string. Watch the tiercel as he sits, a fighting figure of beauty, with eyes as old as time, as glittering as diamonds, on the fist of the falconer fifty yards away, watch him as he is flung, with a lightning flick of the wings into the air, see the upward sweep of that effortless flight until he is high overhead, catch your breath at the sudden sickening stoop as the bird sweeps in a sheer line of beauty straight down the lure, turns on his back, catches it with his talons, loops the loop, flattens out and is away and in the grass, his wings half hooded above his prey, his glittering eyes fixed on his master.

When you have seen such a sight, better still if you have trained a hawk, you will, I think, have seen one of the most stirring and magnificent perfomances in Nature.

That is the high peak of falconry—that and the days when your tiercel takes his first rook, or carrion crow, when your goshawk kills his first hare, or strikes down his first partridge in a sudden shower of fluttering feathers.

But there are the hours wasted when the hawk sits in a tree, full fed and refusing to budge—(Do you remember that old saying, " A fat hawk makes a tired horse, a hungry man, and a lean purse "?)—when you swing the lure minute after minute, all to no purpose. There is the long search when the hawk kills in standing corn and neither tinkle of bell nor movement of the ears of wheat show you where he is. There is the disappointment when, after the first flight and kill of the morning, you realize suddenly that he has wetted his primaries in sodden grass and either refuses to fly or, if he does, is left hopelessly behind.

Worst of all, there is that sickening moment when the bird you have reared and trained disappears over the horizon, never to return.

But these, after all, are the natural drawbacks inherent to any sport worth the name. No disappointment, however bitter, can ever kill the fascination of this game that was old long before the first gun was built.

II

Where Woodcocks dodge, there Distance knows no Laws;
Necessity admits no room for Pause.

GEORGE MARKLAND
Pteryplegia, or, The Art of Shooting Flying

At this time of the year our better-known summer birds prepare to migrate southward and our lesser-known Nature writers sharpen their pencils in anticipation of the booby season in which these dissectors of the avian mind preach annually the doctrine of the intelligence of birds.

We are told year after year at this season that by some marvellous process of thought the swallows prepare to leave this country and arrive eventually, after much transoceanic navigation, at the same kraal in Africa from which they set out seven or eight months ago.

It is pointed out to us with autumnal repetition that certain waders from such parts as Spitsbergen, Franz Josef Land, and Novaya Zemlya arrive in this month on our shores, having accomplished their arduous journey from the Arctic wastes by a sense of aerial navigation unknown to a Cabot, unguessed by da Gama.

The result is that many excellent and sympathetic lovers of bird life, dwelling serenely and unadventurously in the security of their villas, are inclined to regard the arrival or departure of the ordinary autumn migrant as an event most carefully thought out beforehand with meticulous

"Fish-hawk"

" There Distance knows no Laws."

regard to air currents and atmospherics, and eventually accomplished as an object-lesson to the pioneers of modern aviation.

Now, with all respect to the intelligence of the average bird—and I rate it somewhat higher than that of a good many humans I have been privileged to meet—I am none the less of opinion that even the cleverest birds which carry out what are, apparently, the most extraordinarily well-thought-out rules of life and travel are merely creatures of instinct rather than of deliberate reason.

They cannot think. They are the slaves of instinct, a force far greater than the workings of their minute brains.

It has been said that a woodcock possesses a greater brain in relation to its size than any bird in this country. But even if you take the brain of a woodcock and compare it, proportionately, weight for weight, ratio for ratio, with that of gorilla, chimpanzee, horse, dog, cat, or elephant—to take a few of the most intelligent mammals—the result would show that the woodcock's brain counts for very little.

The fact is, as some American writer recently remarked, "birds are born lucky." They enter this life almost completely equipped by Nature to deal with its requirements. Chickens can run within a few minutes of leaving the shell. They can pick for their living immediately.

Ducklings can swim as soon as born. Rooks and eaglets alike can fly within a comparatively short time of their emergence from the shell. No married man can hope to equal their skill in taking short and unsuspected flights from the domestic circle. Moreover, these flights are more often than not rewarded by safety.

In fact, if one were born a bird it would be comparatively common sense to say that one would leap straight from the cradle into the ready-made state of being a fledgling barrister —which Heaven forbid—an incipient stockbroker, which the Devil forfend—or a promising dealer in textiles or tallow. In other words, one would start relatively far higher up the rungs of everyday competition with life than the average human baby.

But beyond those essential, native-born instincts to build, forage, and procreate, the bird's mind does not go. Instinct does everything for it. Indeed, Dr Robert Cushman Murphy, of the American Museum of Natural History, has said: "Birds—even the higher type such as parrots, crows, and song-birds—have very little machinery to think with. Their mental apparatus is more nearly that of an insect than that of a man. Born with a mechanism of instinct, birds do things without knowing why they do them. They live by a chain system of stimuli and responses and we can't realize how stupid they are until, through some mischance, the chain is broken."

Now that may seem very hard language to apply to creatures, which sentimentally we like to regard as possessing a peculiar intelligence of their own. But it is not far short of the mark.

Break the routine of a bird's life and see what happens.

Take an ordinary song-bird with a nest in a hedgerow.

The mother will often fly miles to find food for her young. She will travel over a whole parish, perhaps two parishes, and return unerringly to the same nest, in the same hedge, in the same field.

But move the nest three or four feet and the unhappy bird will fly backward and forward, distracted beyond measure, unable to find its young, flying here and there in a blind, unreasoning, unthinking search. Perhaps finally, after hours of flying backward and forward to the same spot, she will discover the nest simply by the method of trial and error.

Dr Murphy has quoted a case to illustrate the fallacy of the belief that some birds are clean in their nests by habit. Most birds are good housekeepers, if we leave out rooks, herons, and a few others. They do not allow their nests to become befouled. All droppings are carefully removed.

Indeed, one theory is that they are carried away to a safe distance, so that there shall be no tell-tale marks to betray the whereabouts of the nest. Because of this, some observers have become convinced of the high intelligence of such birds.

But recently a group of Cambridge University naturalists watched the nest of twenty 'common birds,' and, according to Dr Murphy, "removed the droppings with tweezers so that they were constantly clean." Dr Murphy goes on to say: "Each time a mother brought a worm for her brood, she took away something on leaving. There were, however, no droppings to be found, so she seized a twig from the nest. It was a mechanical, unreasoning routine—to bring

215

something, to take something away. In time she destroyed the nest."

That perhaps shatters our illusions. But consider the African weaver bird. He builds a nest constructed of material woven and tied into most complicated knots. No old-time sailor could beat the cunning of those intricacies.

For centuries it was thought that each weaver bird taught its young how to tie and weave. But nowadays we rear weaver birds from eggs hatched in incubators. And the young tie the knots on their own—never having seen their parents. Surely that is instinct?

Are birds so intelligent after all? Where, we may ask, does instinct end and reason begin?

BLACKCOCK

216

III

The Gales are gotten up with night;
The stormy West's a-hum,

I hear a grouse-cock's wild " Go Back,"
I see a kindling star
Redden amid the flying wrack
Above the braes of Mar.

PATRICK CHALMERS
Green Days and Blue Days

Englishmen have found a new sport—harpooning the basking shark.

Off the west coast of Scotland and of Ireland, fishermen have been pursuing the shark in dead earnest for centuries. Tiger King and his companions caught a fine specimen in Flaherty's film " Man of Aran." But so far not more than a score of Englishmen have tried this new and, occasionally, arduous sport.

The basking shark is a large, sun-loving, comparatively harmless member of the shark family. I say comparatively harmless because although he does a great deal of damage to fisheries he does not normally attack human beings.

He is a destroyer of food-fish, a terror to the mackerel and herring shoals. His presence on the fishing grounds of the west coast of Scotland may mean the loss of hundreds of pounds' worth of fish to the crofters who go out in their little boats from small whitewashed cottages set on lonely shores.

217

Their nets are hand-made, their boats home-made. Both are rough and ready, tough and reliable. But if a basking shark—anything from nine to forty-five feet in length—strikes one of their nets in pursuit of a shoal of fish, the net has gone in tatters and the boat may even be swamped.

The impact of a fish weighing four and a half tons striking a drifting trawl is enough to pull the bows down into a short sea and to cause her to broach to.

For centuries the basking shark has been a minor danger to fish and fishermen in the western seas of Scotland. Sometimes he has been shot, sometimes taken in nets, occasionally driven ashore.

He is the father of more than half the legends of sea serpents and sea monsters. For nothing looks more like a prehistoric monster than a forty-five foot basking shark, rolling lazily on the surface of a sunlit sea, causing sudden heaves

and splashes on an oily surface beneath one of those mag-
nifying summer mists which drop suddenly off the hills and
spread themselves on the water.

This habit of basking on the surface of the sea, rather as
tench, bream, or carp will bask on the surface of ponds and
rivers, is the undoing of the basking shark. For they can be
harpooned by hand from a boat.

The Isle of Arran, off the Scottish coast, is the centre from
which the new sport is being followed. A fishing-smack has
been fitted out specially there for parties who wish to go out
' sharking.'

The little black fishing-smack plugs steadily along with
chug-chugging engines or sails through polished seas, where
the little islands lie like shining stones.

You may have to cruise about for a day, or maybe even
for five days, before the look-out man spots suddenly what
you are searching for—the dark triangular fin cutting sharply
the scarcely rippled surface of a silent sea.

Lots have been cast beforehand for the privilege of throwing the first harpoon. The lucky man takes his stand in the
bows, harpoon poised, the warp neatly coiled ready to whip
off in coil after coil the moment the barb strikes and the fish
shoots.

It needs a sure eye, a strong arm and a supple wrist to
hurl the big steel head of the harpoon, with its wooden
shaft, eight inches or more into the tough body of the shark.

The harpoon may glance off. The head of it may break
or pull out. The barbs may snap off.

219

Even if the head of the harpoon stands up to the sudden, mad, sideways plunge of the wounded fish the struggle is far from ended. In fact, something like four out of five sharks are lost after they have been harpooned.

Yet the wound made by a hand harpoon on a three- or four-ton shark is not more serious comparatively than a cut finger to a human being. It is nothing compared with the frightful gashes and lacerations which one shark will inflict on another.

But suppose your barb has struck well home. The fish shoots out straight ahead. The rope whips after it, suddenly tightens, taut as a harp string. The fish plugs steadily ahead, whitening the water, thrashing and boring. The smack surges slowly after it.

It is an odd sensation. The shark is actually *towing* a fifty-foot-long ship of at least five times its own weight.

The fight goes on. Gradually the fish tires. Slowly he is hauled in. A slip noose is passed over his tail. It draws tight.

And then the shark is either towed ashore, drowned as the water passes into the gills, or hauled up by the winch until it is half aboard the ship and can be killed with an axe.

Through the still, olive-tinted seas the ship makes for the tiny island harbour, where the little white-washed Highland cottages squat on the water's edge like sea-gulls.

On these seas, in just such a summer twilight, under such a rising moon, beneath the silent, watching faces of the same old mountains, the ancestors of the same gulls quarrelling, the same light mists moistly kissing their faces, the skin-clad Gaels rowed home their great war-canoes two thousand years ago, with the dead shark, the wolf of the sea, trailing in their wake, victim of the hand harpoon.

The fishers of old went out on a deadly errand that to-day has become a sport so new that little more than a score of Englishmen have yet thrown the harpoon.

IV

We wait behind the blackthorn hedge,
        The beaters' slow advance;
Gold sedges hold the sun in pledge,
        A finch's gold wings glance;
Faint-calling partridges afar. . .
        My son, in briefest words,
The roots beyond the stubbles are
        Fair chock-a-block with birds.

PATRICK CHALMERS
Green Days and Blue Days

Flat black fields that run on mile after mile into the horizon; dykes full of brown peat-stained waters; acres of hard green, shiny mangold leaves glistening in the sun; half a mile away the green line of the river-wall where the 'Lode' cuts a ribbon of water across the land, full fifteen feet above the level of the fields.

In the distance the neutral colours of the turf-fen blend into a flat blur of greys and browns, above which snipe drum and the arms of draining mills wave grotesquely.

Ahead of us lie wave on wave of roots, shining flatly in the sun. Cheero, the red wild Irishman, and Fan, fat and matronly, plough and wallow ahead like ships in a green sea, the sunlight striking such notes of colour from dogs and leaves as confound the eye.

Suddenly Cheero stops, drops, and is backed by Fan in her awkward spaniel fashion. We move up, a moment with one's heart in mouth—confound the sun on those leaves!—then *whirr! whirr! whirr!*—a brown shell bursts almost at one's feet, other brown shells fly up in front and to the side, and fifteen birds scatter to three points of the compass.

The sting of nitro, the acrid tang of burnt powder in the nostrils, a vision of feathers blowing by on the wind, Cheero plunging in the roots, head up, ears astray, all nerves and muscles, and one's first brace on the fen are in the bag.

So on through the day with here a snipe, once a teal shot as it sprang from a fen pool, flashing a shower of glittering drops of water, perhaps a brace of flappers dropped out of a brood which jumped strongly from the peat cuttings and, through it, the dominant theme of partridges—partridges in

every odd, unexpected corner, giving every odd, unexpected shot.

Partridges sprung from a dried-up dyke, the hindermost dropped as they fled up between the reed-fringed banks; partridges flushed from the lee of a sedge stack and missed ignobly as they topped its ridge; partridges surprised dusting on the sunny side of a draining mill and snapshotted between the sails—and, of course, that covey which rose thirty yards ahead as one walked the potatoes and, having the blood of immortals in them, came back straight and swift, like black meteors over one's head. *Bang! bang!* a backward swing, starting a foot below the bird, and down they came clattering about your feet.

They were good days, those old rough days on the fen. One walked far and long, leaped dykes and carried one's own bag, shot precious little and never knew what would get up—but what better days are there?

There were, of course, those other days, high festivals, when, a bare dozen miles from the fen, one stood behind the straight-ruled hedges of a Newmarket manor, with the land falling on the left to where the Swaffhams melt into the haze of the fens and, on the right, sweeping up to the skyline of the Dullingham downland and Wesley Waterless—a day on which the sky was cobalt blue, the air was clean with that nip which only 'the Heath' can give, the Gog Magogs were enchanted hills, beaters and flankers worked like an army, one's gun muscles were limber, and a miss was a thing not spoken of among Christian men.

their day was near its end—that they, most aristocratic of all dogs of the gun, were on the threshold of an era which would have no use for them?

You will not find many pointers on the stubble nowadays. Theirs was the day of buskins and muzzle-loaders, of shot flasks and ramrods, of grandfathers in tall hats, drab breeches, and blue waistcoats—good days when your gunner rose at five of the clock, ate fat pork and drank his own home brew for breakfast, put a sandwich of cold bacon as thick as his hand in his pocket, and started out to shoot his manor with no thought of stopping till the sun should swim down in the west.

You will still find men of that sort, albeit they shoot now with breech-loaders, in the lonely parts. You will still find old stranded farms and manors where these men live with horse and gun and a pointer of the old sort. They are good to meet and shoot with, a healthy breath from simpler days. I think the man in the picture must have been of the sort that I knew at High Fen—neither squire nor yeoman, but a blend of both. A thousand-acre man as long as he lived, bred to the old Tory creed of Church and State, a man of fustian and good blood. Everything about the place spoke of the master; horseflesh, stock, crops, and dogs were sound and good. Pointers I think he liked most because of the grace and strength of them, the straight beauty of those firm legs, the depth of chest, the honest width between the eyes, the strength of jaw and the breadth of muscle that meant the best that breeding and brains can put into the form of a dog.

One day stands out above all. We started at six in the morning, the sun glistening on the higher stubbles, struggling with the mist on the lower cattle fens. The old black mill stood up stark out of the fen fog below the stackyard. A skein of mallard from the fen etched straightly their flight above the poplars by the barn. Partridges were calling in the great sixty-acre field beyond where the mangolds billowed away in a green sea; their broad leaves wetted one's gaiters and left glistening drops on Ponto's flanks. In front of me ranged Shot, second of the brace, working on a hundred-yard front. It was pretty shooting on those wide fen fields. You walked in the freshness of morning, the loose black peat crumbling underfoot like coarse sand, the sun sucking up the mists off the level miles; field on field, dyke on dyke, line on line of slim willows, hazing away into the distance where the great lantern on Ely Cathedral shone silver in the morning sun like a palace set upon a hill; brown, peat-stained water gleamed flatly in the dykes; moorhens scuttered up out of the bordering roots and, getting up speed, topped the willows like black woodcock; on the far river wall, against the sky, stood great fen beeves, limned like figures on a fresco. Peewits cried above them, flashing like snowflakes as they turned.

Then, suddenly—stiffened muscles, statuesque limbs, tail like a poker, the whole a blessing to the eye—barely had one time or wit to take in the picture when the covey burst like a shell, cataclysmic, bewildering, speeding a bare yard above the mangold leaves, going like blazes. You got on to the out-

side right bird, crumpled him up, and saw the water flash in a
shower of sun-caught drops as he fell in the dyke.

They swung left, crossing to the 'Master' in his gaiters
and brown cords; there came the glint of sun on gun barrels,
a white opening flower of smoke, the heavy bang of black
powder, and right and left were dropped with pretty skill—
to be gathered from the wet roots, with the blue reek of
smoke a yard above the ground, the smell of burnt powder
stinging the nostrils.

II

To the attentive eye, each movement of the year has its own beauty, and in the same field it beholds, every hour, a picture which was never seen before, and which shall never be seen again.

RALPH WALDO EMERSON
Beauty

Many years ago I was walking home one still October night under a harvest moon, along the marsh wall that bounds Wicken Fen in Cambridgeshire. On the left were the still waters, wreathed in mist, of Wicken Lode. On the right lay the Turf Fens. So that one walked on a great reedy wall of earth with the waters on the left almost level with one's feet, the shrunken fens on the right, a sea of ground mist below one's boots. It was like walking on the edge of two topsy-turvy worlds.

And as I walked there came suddenly, clear and sibilant on the still air of the autumn night, a long low whistle. It was rather like the diminished echo of a train very far away, coming out of a tunnel, so clear, so full, yet so reduced in volume.

And I flopped on my youthful belly among the dew and the reeds. It was wet and cold. I lay still and watched.

And down the waterway, cleaving a clear and V-shaped path across the still surface, brushing silkily through the thin reeds, came a round, bullet-shaped head with large eyes, swimming with an unbelievable ease. It passed me within

234

four feet. In its mouth was a bream, glistening fat and silver in the moon, a good two-pounder. And on the bank opposite, not twenty feet from my nose, the bullet-shaped head with the wake of bubbles behind it steered into the bank. Up the side clambered a wet and glistening form, snaky in the moon-glow.

Once again came that clear, full, low whistle. And out of the reeds bundled three or four agile, playful, kitten-like

forms. They jumped and tumbled, fought and scrambled, seized the fish from their mother, and ate greedily. It was the first time I had seen an otter at close quarters.

For twenty minutes I lay and watched them. And when they had finished their meal they had sliding matches down the bank—one after the other plunging head-first down a muddy chute into the water, to disappear with an almost noiseless plop, leaving a trail of bubbles. Thirty seconds later they would reappear, scramble up the bank, and slide in again —mother and cubs all having the time of their lives.

Since then I have seen a good many otters. I have seen them swimming for dear life before hounds, seen them slipping up the mud of the foreshore on the coast, luminous with phosphorescence on quiet nights in September when the air was alive with the wings of wildfowl. I once had an otter come and play at my feet when I sat in a gun-hole by the side of a marsh fleet, waiting for duck. And the more you see of otters the more you like them.

They are the most intelligent, and probably the most harmless, of all the weasel family. For the otter, oddly enough, is a weasel. He is a blood-brother of the marten and the polecat, the stoat and the weasel. His hide is tougher than that of a fox, but his scent is stronger—that is, to the nose of a hound. But if you hold an otter close to your face you can barely smell it. It entirely lacks the rankness of the fox.

How often has one smelt a fox, foul and heavy on the air, when walking a hedgerow or stealing quietly through a wood. But the otter, almost scentless to the human nose, is so strong

"The more you see of otters the more you like them."

to hounds that they can follow him through marsh, river, and sea-water, through everything indeed that by all the usual laws of Nature should kill scent.

Personally, I hold the view that otters do good to fishing rivers. Otters will rid a river of eels quicker than anything. And the eel is the greatest enemy of trout. He will eat their eggs quicker than any creature on earth, duck and moorhens not excepted. The otter is the only real enemy of the eel. He can swim at probably ten to fourteen miles an hour, which is certainly the fastest speed of which an eel is capable. He can dive to a depth of forty feet. And not many eels live deeper than that in the average river.

Moreover, the otter goes into the dark depths of the streams and there he routs out and devours the old and cannibal trout, the enemies of their own great-great-grandchildren, the hook-nosed brutes whom no fly will ever take.

In fact, I believe it is not far short of the mark to say that an otter is a definite asset on a trout stream. He rids it of eels, cannibals, and weak and sickly fish. When he is eating a fish he eats like a cat, with his eyes half-closed. Usually he leaves the head and the tail.

If he becomes bored with a fish diet he will eat young rabbits, crabs, lobsters, sea anemones, freshwater mussels, and crayfish. Both dabchicks and moorhens are fairly frequently taken, but here again the angler benefits, for both birds are bitter enemies of fish. On the debit side one must admit that otters have been known to kill half-grown pheasants, to devour duck on the nest, and it is even

237

suggested in the Lake district that they will kill very small lambs. It is just possible.

On the other hand, there is a story of an otter cub which lost its mother and night after night cuddled itself up against the side of a lamb in the sheep shippen. This happened on the Trebartha estate in Cornwall in March 1914, and was vouched for by Mr Colwill, the tenant of the farm. The theory was that the otter cub had been suckling itself from the mother sheep.

On the west coast of Scotland, on the wild and rocky shores of the Isles, there are flat rocks here and there worn smooth by the countless feet of hundreds of generations of otters. They are known as ' otters' altars.' For centuries they have been used as dining-tables by the otter on migration. And when an otter has the wanderlust on him he may, and often does, travel hundreds of miles. Neither sea, nor river, nor mountain, nor even the mills, factories, and slums of a great waterside city will stop him.

There have been numerous cases in the last few years of otters being caught and killed when passing up the polluted streams of Lancashire and Yorkshire, such as the Wharfe and the Aire. They were merely following the paths of their ancestors, the old trackways that existed hundreds of years before the mills were built, the slums came, and the chemicals poisoned the waters of what once were wild and tumbling mountain streams.

And the otter will be swimming up those streams again when chemicals no longer poison them.

238

III

SANDRINGHAM . . . has preserved the old and simple things, the loveliness of fields and woods, the accumulated beauty of centuries.

Here, where time treads slowly and the sea winds are free of smoke, where great woods still stand brilliant against dun ploughland, where the uplands melt into the marshes and the marshes meet the sea, there lingers something of the spirit and the beauty which bred the old England of the squire and the yeoman, the England of individuals and not of masses.

J. WENTWORTH DAY
King George V as a Sportsman

I was brought up among great shots. It is no boast, since I shoot indifferently. But on the threshold of memory in those golden days of the nineteen hundreds the great shot was not uncommon, the good shot moderately plentiful. Men had more leisure and more money. Rather shall I say that the money was in the hands of those who appreciated good shooting and were brought up to it. The rural horizon was serene and unblemished save for an impending thundercloud from Wales named Lloyd George.

Partridge manors were broad and well-keepered. They were shot, not by syndicates of week-ending persons in effulgent checks, but by their native squires. The country gentleman was not yet condemned to a third-floor flat in Bayswater, and the manufacturer had not assumed that titular lordship of the soil which to-day accompanies a gun in an agent's shoot.

239

Brightest of the shooting stars in our East Anglian firmament was Tom de Grey, sixth Lord Walsingham.

He dominates those childhood memories, a most terrific and frightening figure clad in garments more amazing than even the eccentricities of a pre-war mind could devise. On his head he wore a cap made from the skin of a hedgehog. The spines stuck out like pins in a pincushion. The snout and grinning teeth were pulled down over his eyes as a peak. Above gleamed two black beady eyes. His waistcoat was of snakeskin. His jacket was of moleskin, black and shining like the silkiest velvet. Below were cords and the old sort of buskins that did up in the front.

This, let me premise, was not his normal shooting attire. On orthodox days he wore black and white checks on which a whole Economic Conference could have played noughts and crosses. But he wore his snake and moleskin when he came to my old home at Wicken, on the edge of the old, wild, undrained fens, where the bittern still booms to-day, where the Montagu harrier still nests in the reed beds, where he and my uncle, the late Isaac Aspland, who owned the hind legs of Robert the Devil, and the late Frederick Johnson, of Wicken Hall, and the late William ('Longbow'—because he drew it) Howlett, of Barton Mills, once killed as many snipe on a winter's morning as would fill a bushel measure.

I doubt if we shall ever see Lord Walsingham's like again. His fame to-day rests on that amazing bag made at Bluberhouses on August 30, 1888, when, using a pair of hammer guns, he killed 1070 grouse with 1510 cartridges in a day.

not perhaps saying too much to suggest that the estate in those days was run perhaps a little lavishly. It was the late King's pet property and no money was spared.

The Duke of Windsor is a very fine shot indeed, a fact for which he is seldom or never given credit, but he heartily dislikes easy shooting and big bags.

"I have stood behind him at Sandringham and seen him let half a dozen pheasants fly overhead in succession without even raising his gun at them. They were too easy. But when a real high bird came over, with the wind in his sails and going like steam, King Edward had him down in a twinkle." Those were the words of a Sandringham keeper who has seen the Duke grow up from a small boy. He added: "I have seen his Majesty hand his gun to a friend and tell him to get on with the shooting because the birds were too easy. But just let him be faced with one of those old cocks that come curling down-wind with a sideways swerve on—one of the most difficult shots of all—and the King was on him like lightning."

King George VI is extremely interested in shooting and shoots more than well. He is easily the best shot in the Royal Family and well on the way to being among the best in all England. A Norfolk loader, whom I had last season, straight from Sandringham, told me that the King's stance and swing was almost identical with that of his father in his earlier days as Prince of Wales. The old man has loaded at Sandringham for thirty years. Some time ago, when I had the honour of dining privately with his Majesty, the talk for two hours was of shooting and nothing else. He told me that the holiday which had pleased him most and would remain in his memory longest was his *safari* in the Lake Rukwa region of Tanganyika some few years ago—a remote and little visited area full of game.

GODWIT

NOVEMBER

I

But now there comes and comes and comes to me
The crooning and the murmur of the sea,
An hour before the dawn, at flighting time,
—A winter dawn—my greatcoat white with rime—
When, crouching low behind the grey sea-wall,
I waited for the geese, and heard their call.

W. G. M. DOBIE
Flighting

I STOOD in the bitter air of Norfolk sandhills, on an evening when sea and wind filled the world. Behind, beyond the black woods of Holkham, the sun died in a last balefire of red and amber. In front, the sullen seas that moved tremulous from Iceland to the Wash murmured on the sand. And over their bottle-green crests, green beneath the apple-green of a twilight sky, there flitted in from sea a bird.

He lit in the Marram grass almost at my feet, weary and unafraid, so weary that all fear was dead. And there in the face of the sandhills, in the bitter wind of the sea, where the breath of winter marched on the frost, he slept—a woodcock from abroad.

With his long bill tucked into his breast, the colour of autumn leaves, his liquid eyes shrouded in sleep, he looked very different from the woodcock who laughs at the guns and leave the best of them ejecting useless cartridges.

He was the first that I have seen come in, wing-weary from nine hundred miles of Scandinavian voyaging. And if you have eyes, wit, and a little luck, you will see many another small Columbus light on our shores from voyages that would put Cabot and Mercator to shame.

I dare say that woodcock came from Holland. He may have taken off from some wet and distant Brabantine willow-holt. He may have touched land last among the bleak dunes of Terschelling, or left the strong-smelling pine woods of Mecklenburg, a distant memory. But I like to think that when he lit, small and unafraid, at my feet, he had come from the shores of the great lakes of Wener and Wetter, or per-haps from some Norwegian scree where the blaeberries are nipped with the frost and the ryper crouch on the snow-line.

And that night, as I sat beneath my roof of East Anglian thatch, I heard above, in the frosty silence of the sky, the voice of geese. They came baying, like Valkyriean hounds, the skeins of the brent, the black geese of the gunners that cluster in their clanging thousands on the mud-flats of St Peter's, the sand-bars of the Buxey, and the Gunfleet.

Two thousand miles by steppe and tundra, by floe and fjord, by mountain and seaway, they came. Kolguev and Novaya Zemlya saw their birth in the all-too-brief green glory of an Arctic summer. The white fox and the eagle owl, the Weddell seal and the killer whale knew their early adventuring.

And when the first whitening cloud came down from the north, when the lichens shrivelled and the fox changed his

" The black geese of the gunners."

coat to driven snow, the geese took wing. They came south by the old seaways that knew Erik the Red. And they passed over my home in the windy silence of the night, a thousand strong, the voyagers of two thousand miles.

And when I shoot pheasants in the deep, warm, fir coverts of a Norfolk manor that I love, I see flitting between the tree stems, stealthy as mice, sudden as jewels, the golden-crested wren. No larger than a florin, if you like easy comparisons, but he may have left Norway to come to Norfolk. The old folks will tell you that they travel on the back of an owl, hid snug in the feathers between the wings. Or perhaps on the back of a crane or a stork. The tale-tellers are not particular.

But as neither crane nor stork come often to England since Vermuyden drained the fens, you may reckon it was an owl.

I like that story. And, though it is easy to like, there are some who do not doubt it. Buffon believed it. Patterson thinks it probable. My friend, Mr Frohawk, is no sceptic. After all, woodcock carry their young between their legs, so why should not an owl, easy of wing and effortless as a moth, carry in its ample feathers a shy and small adventurer scarcely an ounce in weight?

As for the sort of owl, I dare say it was one of these lordly 'Dutch owls' that I shall see on my bleak sea-marsh any winter day.

Be sure that if field mice were plentiful in summer, if rats run riot in the stacks, there will be short-eared owls on all the coastal marshes all the winter until March. Even as the gigantic eagle owls follow the lemmings in Norway, follow by some strange scent or instinct which carries a message of food a hundred miles, so the Dutch owls come to England each winter in greater or lesser numbers as the rats and mice may be small or great in multitude.

Eight of them swung about my head in one day as we walked the fleets and dykes for snipe and teal—eight of them like small and swinging eagles against the hard blue of a winter sky.

And, I think, in all that winter I saw no lovelier sight.

And this winter, if I am lucky, I may see on Forth or Findhorn the coming of a mightier bird—the great snowy owl, fit to kill a hare, white as a ghost and as dreadful. Or I may see, perhaps, as I saw ten years ago, the sudden, unafraid vision of an eagle owl, three feet or more in height, horned like a demon, with yellow eyes burning like a leopard's in the night.

There, if you like, is a bird, the *Grand Duc* of the old French fowlers, who fears nothing on legs or wing, man included. You will not come across him often in England, but in Norway where the elk move mysterious in scarred and ancient woods you may see him brooding in the great pines. He knows the lonely marshes of Masurian lakes where still the phantom armies of the Tsar fall beneath the grey ghosts of German regiments. Like the swans that trumpet on East Anglian estuaries, he knows the fens that heard the thunder of Tannenberg. He is one in habitat with the geese and the swans, the golden-crested wren and the woodcock—but we, to our loss, see him too seldom.

And there is one other bird, small and lowly, a grubber in the mud, his body no larger than a florin, who spans half the world in one breath-taking arc.

When my punt creeps up to the geese in winter, when we stalk the widgeon in the white of the frost, the birds that will fling suddenly from sand-bank and mud-flat, spill like a shower of falling silver across the creeping sea—these are the dunlin, some of whom left African beaches to feed on English mud.

They girdle the earth, cross the continents, and fly the seas, these 'Globe spanners,' as Abel Chapman named them. Almost the smallest bird, like the knot and the curlew sandpiper, they fly the longest distance.

The impulses of migration on the European bird routes

DUNLIN

253

are dimly guessed at. But what godlike courage sends these small morsels to span the globe is more than we know. Which is why I seldom shoot a dunlin—though ten of them in a pie with a little beef-steak and a kidney are so very good that I am almost glad they left Africa.

There are other small birds of a more homely sort, who travel almost as far. Not long since I waited for flighting duck in a reed bed on my marsh on the East Coast at six o'clock on an autumn morning.

It was one of those still, grey mornings, when the tide creeps in like silk, the eastern sky is pale dove-colour with one streak of apple-green—one of those quiet mornings when the sun swims up above the edge of the sea, a drowned ghost.

It scarcely seems that there could, or should, ever be much noise or movement in such a world. The silence is quietly insistent, a large silence, full of the width and height of early morning sky, the stillness of a crawling dawn sea.

No wind stirred. The bark of a dog at a lonely farm on the uplands came clear and distinct across two miles of cattle marsh, creek, and mud-flats.

And in this immense quietness, in this grey, still world, where neither light nor shade was finite, where land and sea seemed fused, there came suddenly to my ears a faint high twittering, far up in the sky.

They were coming in from the sea.

High over the long grey miles of the North Sea, over the mouth of the great estuary which swam like a river of silver between its low, dun uplands, up the crawling creek to the reed bed, where I stood silent in a world of changing browns and gold, the colours turning from summer into late autumn, they came twittering and chacking.

A host of little birds.

Their last resting-place had been scarred and lonely pines in some forest of Scandinavia, where the elk move by day, primeval ghosts between the tree trunks, and the great eagle owl, horned and hooded like a dreadful witch, hunts by night.

They planed in low over the reeds, dropping over the sea-wall like a shower of falling penny pieces, plunging into the blackthorn hedge by the old marsh barn in a perfect hooroosh of wings and voices.

And there, in the baring branches where the last leaves are now turning from green to golden red, where the hips and haws hang like little red lanterns, they settled down to sleep with a tremendous shuffling, chattering, rustling, and chittering.

They were fieldfares and redwings.

You will see them all over England in autumn and winter. They are the hardiest and farthest travelling of all the thrush family, with the possible exception of the missel-thrush, the stormcock of the old country people, that grand, bold fellow, with the strongly speckled front, biggest of all the thrushes.

You will see him, long before spring has unlocked the ice, perched at the top of a tall tree, swaying in the wind, pouring out a wild and broken song, one instant clear and high, the next drowned in the sough of the wind.

255

But whereas the missel-thrush is with us all the year round, the fieldfares and redwings, those wary, gregarious, adventurous cousins, arrive in autumn in their thousands.

FIELDFARE

They are creatures of the big open fields, eaters of grubs and worms, good friends of the farmer, a high peak of autumn bird life.

You will know a fieldfare because he is about the size of a missel-thrush.

He has a speckled breast, but the feathers on his cheeks and at the back of his eyes are pale dove-grey—like the dove-grey of that sky against which they came in when I saw them.

There is a dash of burnt red on the shoulders and across the back, and then at the base of the long bold tail, more soft grey, dove-like feathers, until the straight dark tail-feathers shoot out into that rudder which has guided him over seas and forests to his bourne.

At the back of his eye, running down in front of the shoulders, is a boldly marked black pencilling—altogether a very handsome fellow.

You can tell fieldfares when they are on the wing because they nearly always fly in flocks, and that harsh, insistent *chack! chack! chack!* is not quite like the cry of any other bird in Britain.

Male and female are very much alike in colour, and the song, such as it is, was well described by that great naturalist Seebohm as " a wild, desultory warble."

Their first cousins, the redwings, which come with them, are not so striking in plumage. There is none of that soft dove-grey.

Indeed, you might almost take them to be ordinary song-thrushes (I like better the word ' mavis ' we used when I was a boy) if it were not for that brilliant dash of red on the wing which gives them their name.

They, too, like the great open pastures where the sheep move in woolly, undulating seas; where the curlew come to feed at high tide; where the magpies gather in sixes and tens. (In October I saw thirty-three all together, a number so portentous that I opened my newspaper the next morning confident of a second Adowa.)

R   257

The redwings and the fieldfares like the bare open fields because of the wireworms, the grubs, and all the horrid little insects that make a farmer's life a burden.

When the weather is sharp they go into the hedges, the holts, the shaws, and the copses—into any of those little clumps of trees and bushes which you can call by any of these names, according to the part of England to which you belong.

They go there for berries; the little red Chinese lanterns that make the bushes gay when the boughs are black and the wind-driven snow sticks white and icy on the weather side.

And then, about April, when autumn is a memory and winter a laggard ghost, when spring comes soft and soppy, the fieldfares and the redwings gather in their immensities and decide that England is no longer a land for hard-living folk.

So off they go back to Scandinavia. Sympathize—but before they go the redwings, or, at any rate, the cocks, gather in little parties of from ten to fifty or sixty and sing to each other.

They, the troubadours of winter, who through all the long cold months have lived and sung like soldiers, gather then, singing to themselves. They sing very low and soft and quietly.

The chorus is so subdued that you may stand fifteen yards away and never hear it.

I stood one April in a little holt of wind-twisted black-thorns, under a sea-wall, with a thousand brent geese cronking on a far-out mudbank like the gabble of a distant football crowd, while in the branches a few yards above my head—I was in a grass pigeon-' hide '—fifteen cock red-wings sang to each other a little gentle song that only just reached my ears.

I dare say they were telling each other what a terrific voyage it would be all the way to Norway, and what a grand girl they were taking with them—that life, after all, was well worth living when you could live all the winter like a storm-cock, swing on a high tree like a king of the winds and con-quer the oceans twice in a twelvemonth.

For that is what the fieldfares and the redwings do.

So when you see them sitting out in the middle of the big cattle pastures, pecking unconcernedly among the bullocks, or moving with the curlews and the jackdaws among the roving sheep, when they flight high and bold above your country road, or come with a swoop and a rush into the thick plantation or the little lonely marsh holt at night, raise your mental wig to them—the jolly and gallant troubadours of winter.

II

Oh! it is great to shake off the trammels of the world and of public opinion—to lose our . . . personal identity in the elements of Nature, and become the creature of the moment, clear of all ties.

William Hazlitt

Last Sunday I sailed in a small open yawl, with homely red sails, to a small island on the East Coast. It is a mile in circumference, a place of tussocky marsh and gleaming fleets. It is set in the shining waters of an estuary that has changed little since the Danish galleys rode there at anchor. And this lonely little island is marked on all maps as a place without a house.

Yet when we landed and walked through staring bullocks to the few wind-blown oaks, the stunted thorns, which are the only standing trees on the island, we found there a house. It is built of wood and has three rooms. And in it live a man and his wife, who have seen quite a little of this world.

But for thirty years they have lived nine months of the year on the island, bringing even their drinking water from the mainland in beakers. They have left civilization, newspapers, politics, noise, mortgages, overdrafts, and the other obvious amenities of civilization safely anchored on the mainland half a mile away. They are alone with the rabbits and the bullocks, the mournful curlew and the creeping tides.

260

It is, I suppose, surprising to reflect that there are more than sixty islands within sixty miles of London. And the most individual people live on them. Mr Compton Mackenzie has a pretty taste in them. But he goes too far afield.

I like my islands close at hand. They are then all the greater discoveries, the more amazing revelations. There is not only that lonely island of last Sunday where the son of the first mate of the *Cutty Sark*—he was mate when she won her first great tea race—lives with his wife, but there are the other islands.

There is Foulness at the mouth of the Thames, only thirty-five miles from London where, until the war, no person on the island, except the schoolmaster and the parson, had been in a train, and none had ever seen a soldier in uniform. There was not even a road to Foulness when I knew it first. There is Potton next door to it, a place seven miles in circumference, with only two trees on it, a plum-tree and a damson, only two houses, three inhabitants, no roads and no fresh water.

But the big house was built by Nicholas Van Cropenborough in 1630. So why worry if you had to bring your water in barrels by boat? There was Rushley next door, and Wallasea, which was depopulated when farming became a joke.

And in the Blackwater estuary, fifteen miles farther north, there is Northey, where the last raven to nest in Essex hatched its eggs in 1866.

Victor De Crespigny held Northey for years. The fishermen used to come and poach on it. And Victor used to issue from his farmhouse door in his nightshirt and shoot at them with a Service revolver—but purposely very wide of the mark. And when he caught them he would have a fight with bare fists. After that they all went indoors and tapped the big barrels in the kitchen corner.

And below Northey, towards the sea, is Osea, where the Danes had their war camp. After the Danes came F. N. Charrington. He constructed there a gaudy architectural receptacle for inebriates. He filled it with sodden wrecks. And the greatest bootlegging trade in England sprang up. Sometimes the drunks would tumble into dinghies and float blissfully on an understanding tide up the river to the waterfront public-houses of Maldon. And thence, late in the evening, wafted by the hand of God and an ebbing tide, they would return, without conscious volition, to the austere shores of Osea, their pockets charged with the illicit gods of their devotion.

But sometimes it was not always easy thus to invoke wind and water. The drunks remained marooned. And to them came the fishermen, who stole ashore under cover of dusk, and, with a rude simplicity inherited from Danish forbears, sold them raw whisky that would drive a train, at thirty shillings a bottle. It was planted in the haystacks and the cornricks, in hollow trees, in pigsties, and in fields of standing corn. And the climax of the joke was to see the other drunks, those who had done no bartering, prowling the fields next morning, searching the trees and stacks, robbing their brethren of the bottles they had paid for. These hi-jackers were a fearful race.

To-day there are no drunks on Osea, but equally there are no rats, no snakes, and no foxes. Which is, perhaps, why you can kill a brace of birds to the acre. Mr Bunting, who has four hundred years of Essex yeomen stock behind him, is lord of Osea to-day. And he will not let you land.

Round the corner, round the fifteen salty miles of tide-race, of mud-flat and shoal, fairway and shallows, there lies another island, the island on which no man dare build a house. That is the Ray.

The Ray is at the back of Mersea. It is a place of long rough grasses, full of adders and rabbits, crowned by a witch-like grove of storm-stunted thorn-trees, where the carrion crow croaks. And no one has ever dared to build a house there. For it is haunted by footsteps. If you camp there in a tent, as did Mr Ivan Pullen of Peldon, you will hear, in the height of the bright moon, footsteps marching all about you. They marched even into Mr Pullen's tent. And although he had a gun, is marsh-born, and has sailed the North Sea for thirty years, Mr Pullen ran for his boat.

Baring-Gould told the story of the ghost of the Ray in *Mehalah*. It is a ghost that has come down from the Romans, the restless footsteps of the Centurion who lies buried there, the lost leader of the eagles who marches every night on his beat inspecting his ghostly sentinels. So you see that even an Island without a house has none the less its Individual.

III

You're vermin to a vast of folk, but glory to a few.
What is it in your creeping stride that calls and calls
    and calls?
What is it, when the racing pack runs on from scent
    to view,
That rallies us to ride our best—dead straight—and
    chance the falls?

WILL. H. OGILVIE
Our Pilots

I sat the other night by a lake, coot-haunted, in a park of the old sort, full of jackdaw oaks, fishing for bream on a slow and lethargic line. It was midnight. And you do not, if you are normal, commonly fish for bream at midnight. But so much can happen at the twelfth hour when the moon is up that it is worth sitting on your behind in a wet and rheumatic state in order to listen.

You must, if you have a good imagination, see my lake. There are the reeds with the mist about their feet, the moon a little pale through these autumn fogs that creep up from the marshy parts like thin ghosts not yet quite sure of themselves. There are the great oaks. There are the coots clanking on the mere, those solemn, bald-headed birds. A coot is the true counterpart of a monk, in spirit and in setting. Can you imagine a fish stew complete without its coot?

And there are the owls. There is the little owl, mewing

in a melancholy fashion from the sheltered solitude of a pollard oak, full of holes, fit to shelter his murderous soul. There is the barn owl, wide-eyed, delicately tawny, delicately white, a wraith-like creature, of age and dignity, snoring

from his hole in the very old oak that stands, a sad and solitary sentinel, beneath the stable gates of this house where I fished for bream. Its gables and twisted chimneys, its long mullions and cupolas rise above a park that at this hour is knee-deep in mist, musical with the quiet, mysterious presence of owl, coot, and fox.

Which brings me to the subject of this story. As I sat in the reeds fishing for my unimaginative bream, a dog-fox barked behind me. And of a sudden, all the old, old voices that had been heard in that park for hundreds of years were crystallized into the voice of the fox. For the fox is an individual: not only an object of pursuit.

There is a lot to be said for him. He circulates £4,500,000 a year in England alone. No less than one hundred and ninety-three packs of hounds hunt him in the British Isles. He has survived the stag, the wolf, the boar, the bear—all the noble beasts were creatures of far greater account than the miserable, crawling, vermin fox.

Let me give you the bald details of his build, comportment and demeanour. The average dog-fox weighs fifteen pounds, and a vixen weighs a pound and a half less. The lightest fox ever killed is supposed to have tipped the scale at only eleven pounds. And the heaviest, so far as my records go, was killed by the Ullswater on Cross Fell a few years ago. It weighed twenty-three pounds and measured fifty-two inches from nose to tip of brush. The last four inches of the brush were pure white.

Last year the Coniston Hounds killed an 18½ lb. dog-fox who was four feet and half an inch over all, which is pretty good. The Ullswater during the same season killed a sixty-five inch fox whose weight was not recorded.

These Fell foxes are inclined to run much larger and bigger than our English foxes. Differences of climate, country, and food account for the variations in size and length.

But, wherever you may find him, the fox still remains a most intelligent, irritating, defeating, and enchanting creature. He is commonly accused of low cunning. That,

I think, is the refuge of the defeated. I would suggest that he has a distinctly higher intelligence.

His drawback is that, although Nature has given him a brain superior to most wild animals, she has also gifted him with scent-glands of the most embarrassing nature. For example, the fox carries a scent-gland beneath his tail. He has also sweat-glands in the pads of his feet and under his skin. When nervous or excited his scent becomes intensified. If a fox chose to lie down in close cover, hounds could work close past him and never smell him, but the moment he is up and off his scent intensifies and betrays him. It weakens when he is beaten. A dead fox scarcely smells at all, and a half-dead fox stands a good chance of escape.

I dare say these theories will upset a few of the orthodox hunting people, who have never troubled to regard the fox as anything except a distant object to be viewed between the ears of a horse. But the test of the pudding is in the eating. If you ask the reason why fox-hunting is popular, I would reply because of its very uncertainty. You will always know where hounds meet, but you can never say where they will be blown off. You can hunt this morning in any country you like, and finish to-night thirty miles away in any direction if your fox, your wind, and your horse will stand it. The fox throws out a challenge to every one who hunts him. He sustains that challenge.

He is built for speed on the most graceful lines, with a hare foot and a sloping pastern which, with those beautifully built shoulders, would make the perfect racehorse if one could breed and copy them. The fox, with hair between his toes, can travel over places where the best-bred hound that ever came out of Berkeley or Beaufort could never hope to follow. A hill fox will go up an almost perpendicular ice-slope.

Some people say that when a fox is beaten he trails his brush. I have never seen it in my own short experience, and I know no one, including men of many years more knowledge, who can speak to it with truth. But he uses his brush as a balancing pole when he is descending a steep hillside, as a rudder when jinking at speed on land or when swimming in water, and as a muff for his face when he is asleep. And he is the most agile creature in England. A squirrel has nothing on a fox.

If a fox makes up his mind to charge through men, horses, and hounds in order to reach home, he will do so. He is far more intelligent than the average hound, and considerably quicker in the uptake than the average fox-hunter. I know: I was brought up among both.

The fox is a good swimmer, and likes the water. He will eat anything you like to give him, from the most stinking carrion that ever affronted the wind to a nest of young rabbits, a turkey, a roe-deer fawn, a partridge on the nest, a chicken in the coop, or even a full-grown and rather elderly sheep on the Fells of the Lake District. Some of those Cumberland hill-foxes, the Greystoke foxes, as they used to call them, are real terrors. They will eat anything.

All these facts are, I think, in favour of the fox. He is a

very artful and resourceful person. He can travel faster than the average hound, climb a hill much quicker, think twice as decisively, act on the spur of the moment, eat anything that comes his way. He is *almost* cleverer than either man or hound. Only the glands of scent and sweat defeat him. But the fox, of course, is not aware of it.

DECEMBER

I

Whither, midst falling dew,
While glow the heavens with the last steps of day,
Far, through their rosy depths, dost thou pursue
    Thy solitary way?

Seek'st thou the plashy brink
Of weedy lake, or marge of river wide,
Or where the rocking billows rise and sink
    On the chafed ocean-side?

WILLIAM CULLEN BRYANT
To a Waterfowl

I n the heart of a wood of pines and firs, their trunks reddened by the sun, lies the pond. Two and a half acres of water still and burnished as a sheet of beaten silver, its shores ringed by screen fences of reed hurdles. At each corner radiate semicircular pipes, channels of water narrowing towards their farther ends. The pipes are arched by gigantic iron hoops covered with netting.

Half a mile away lie the broad waters and strong-smelling mud-flats of a Suffolk estuary. There the widgeon feed on the *zos* grass, the geese flight from sand-bar to mud horse in their clanging thousands, and the coots cover the winter waters in black armadas.

On this quiet pond, in the ancient wood, within sea-smell of the tidal flats, they still practise the oldest art of taking wild duck. Most of the duck that swing in the hard electric light from the hooks of London poulterers are caught on such secret ponds by methods that were old when Charles II was king.

There are not more than a dozen decoy ponds in Great Britain to-day. A hundred years ago there were more than sixty. They were not only the ornaments but the highly profitable appanages of a great estate.

Their annual value sometimes was as great as the rent of a 900-acre farm. Special laws, stringent in their punishment, were passed to protect them. Those laws exist to-day. For instance, you may not fire a gun within a quarter of a mile of a decoy pond without incurring severe penalties.

Their secrets were jealously guarded. The arts of decoying were handed down from father to son. Decoymen ran in dynasties. They still do so to this day.

Two years ago I was able to work a decoy pond at Orwell Park, Suffolk, and take photographs of the decoy pond, one of the best and most valuable in the whole country.

We came to it by a sandy road, through a wood of silver birch and old pines. We trod silently, the decoy man in his corduroy breeches, velveteen jacket, and leather buskins, walking ahead. At his heels padded a small reddish-brown, foxy-looking mongrel, the ' piper.'

Pipers are of no known breed, but they are invaluable. You never see them on a show bench, and they are not in the Stud Book. Almost any good small mongrel will make a piper.

Below us lay the pond, silent in the winter sunlight, bur-

" While glow the heavens with the last steps of day."

nished beneath the hard blue of a frosty sky. In the centre and round the edges there swam, paddled, and dived a vast congregation of all sorts and conditions of wildfowl, a quacking, clanging, gabbling, feeding congregation of ducks to gladden the eye of any naturalist. Mallard, teal, widgeon, pochard, tufted duck, and others of the common sort swam and fed together.

Silently, behind green mossy banks, in a trench full of the sodden leaves of dead and rusty bracken, we circled half the pond until down another trench we approached the mouth of one of the pipes. The wind blew directly towards us.

Holding lumps of burning peat to our mouths—to kill

"Fish-hawk"

TUFTED DUCK

the human scent—we crept towards the reed-screened mouth of the pipe. Fifty yards out a group of twenty mallard rested on the water. They were the tame decoy duck. With a shrill whistle the decoy man threw a handful of corn into the water. It was the feeding call.

The decoy birds suddenly awoke and swam, gaggling and quacking, to the mouth of the pipe. A group of wild birds farther out followed them. We threw more corn over the screens, retreating gradually up the narrowing pipe, hidden from their view by the reed screen.

When they were twenty yards within the mouth of the pipe the decoy man motioned silently to the piper. The little dog wagged his tail, darted between the screens, trotted up a little path by the pipe head, leaped over a low ' dog-jump ' made of reeds, and disappeared from the ducks' view.

We rewarded him with a piece of cheese.

Up went every head, and the ducks swam, quacking and gaggling, up the pipe. They had seen, or thought they had seen, their hereditary enemy the fox. And it is the habit of wild duck to mob the fox when they are on the water, even as rooks will mob and stoop at him in an open field.

Several times the dog appeared and disappeared. And the ducks swam on after him.

When they were safely round the bend I suddenly showed myself behind them. In an instant they were up, quacking frantically, flying and swimming in a confused mass down the narrowing tunnel. At the far end there was no more water and they piled helter-skelter into a long tunnel net

stretched on the ground. The end of the net was dis-
connected and dropped behind them. And there they were,
twenty-six mallard and widgeon, safely imprisoned.

Quickly, silently, the decoy man took them out one by
one, wrung their necks with the flick of a wrist and threw
them into a sack. Thus Leadenhall gets its wild duck.

This art of decoying is at least four or five hundred years
old. It was imported to this country from Holland. Sir
William Wodehouse established the first decoy in England
at Winterton in Norfolk in the seventeenth century, and
Charles II followed with a duck decoy on the island in St
James's Park lake, which he worked for the delight of his
ladies when they hung singing birds in golden cages from
the plane-trees where now is Birdcage Walk.

In the winter of 1918 the Orwell Park decoy took over
10,000 wildfowl. In most years it averages 5000.

II

I like the pheasants and feeding things
    Of the unsuspicious morn;
I like the flap of the wood-pigeon's wings
    As she rises from the corn.

I like these things and I like to ride
    When all the world is in bed,
. To the top of the hill where the sky grows wide,
    And where the sun goes red.

I covet not a wider range
    Than these dear manors give;
I take my pleasures without change,
    And as I lived I live.

WILFRED SCAWEN BLUNT
The Old Squire

A certain politician, who was born a townsman, sits for an industrial constituency, and has never handled a gun, thrown a fly, or sat a horse in his life, pitched this considered bombshell into the placid world of my rural philosophy: " Sport is finished now that the farmer has become a business man. Barbed wire began it and the tractor and electrical farming will finish it."

We were discussing the future of fox-hunting, of which, incidentally, my friend knows nothing. Perhaps that is why, being a Member of Parliament, he laid down the law on the subject with a finality which almost left me stunned.

Actually, that particular M.P. is on a Parliamentary

Advisory Committee which is dealing with the town-planning of rural areas. According to the colour of his votes he is Conservative. But I have never heard such pure Socialism, such abysmal ignorance of the merest elements of country life from any man other than a Socialist tub-thumper.

Yet there are quite a lot of people who believe that the modern farmer should be too busy to have time for sport. They regard hunting, fishing, coursing, shooting, even the ferreting of a few rabbits as a waste of time, a childish indulgence. They cannot conceive that these things can possibly go hand-in-hand with the direction and development of a great industry.

What are the facts? Let us regard them in the light of history. Quite apart from any patriotic trumpet-blowing, the British farmer has been, and still is, the first in the world. Whatever he has produced has been good. His methods have never been equalled. To-day they are still unsurpassed.

I realize that to state this flatly is to ask for the sneers and polite eye-lifting of all the clever self-appointed prophets and reformers who din into our ears each day the news that the Argentine beef producer, the American prairie farmer, the Continental *petit culturist*, and the Russian wheat grower are so much more advanced in their methods, so much more practical in their application, than ourselves. It is usually added that we are able to equal none of these because, firstly, we are unbusinesslike, and, secondly, we waste too much time on sport.

279

What is the truth of the matter? It is this. Two hundred years ago England was breeding the finest sheep, cattle, and horses in Europe. She was growing the best wheat, oats, barley, and roots. She has done so ever since. She is doing so to-day.

The United States, Canada, the Argentine, Australia, and the Continent have founded their studs, flocks, and herds on the pedigree stock exported from this country.

That stock was bred and raised by country squires and yeoman farmers. It was the product of the thought, care, organization, and efficiency of men who have hunted the fox, shot their partridges, coursed their own hares, and filled in their January Saturdays by ferreting rabbits. Like everything else that is good and English, permanent and sound, these things have been founded on the robust common sense which comes from an active body, a healthy mind, a sense of humour, and a simple-minded joy in the sports of the field. You cannot breed a good man without fresh air and hard exercise, without sport to leaven his labours, to lighten his mind.

It is when men are confined in towns with their noses to the pavements, their minds soured by the encompassing prisons of bricks and mortar, of streets and tram-lines, that their livers become out of order, their souls revolt, and their philosophy of life becomes tainted with the rancour of revolt.

But the British farmer, the man who works and lives on the land and by the land, who at the present time is fighting his way out of the worst storm that his industry has ever known, has kept his soul. He still has some vestige of a sense of humour. He still keeps his job going—while the gods promise all and fulfil precious little.

I cannot foresee any future for farming in which sport will not play the accustomed and vital part that it has played for a thousand years. It is impossible to imagine a day when the farmer will become a sort of soulless mechanic, a cross between a robot and an accountant, a grim, unpleasing fellow, a mongrel by Tractor Wheels out of Factory Lass.

No man whose forbears have lived on the land can entirely resist the feel of a gun, the voice of hounds, the note of a horn, the dimple of a rising fish in May, the electric beauty of a pair of long-dogs and a hare, the quick thrill of the wings of fighting duck heard suddenly in the dusk of winter when the salt smell of the sea is strong, and the December wind runs through the reeds, crisps the cold waters of the fleet. These things are part of the blood and bone of mankind. They are older than Rome or Phoenicia. They began with time. They will outlast history.

Even if the farmer of the future is recruited by some fantastic 'five-year plan' from the factory-bred masses of the towns, there will still be within him some far-off, latent spark of these things which will germinate when once his foot takes root in soil of his own. Some old sense of beauty, smothered, perhaps, beneath a century of towns and slums, will wake again.

And usually when a man sees beauty he sees it in terms

translated into the sports of the field. Most of us who shoot remember our partridge days by the colours in fields, the soft mists of early autumn, the sudden flame of changing leaves in the hedgerows, white clouds in a sky as of bird's-egg blue, the glint of the sun on green seas of mangold leaves.

We have seen ' the finest view in Europe ' between the ears of a horse, hounds streaming away across some peewit-haunted pasture with shock-headed willows standing like hairy gnomes by the crawling brook, the dun sweep of winter up-lands running on and up to a skyline heavy with homing rooks.

Do we forget the green silences of the stream in May, when the cattle stand in the shallows, tails swishing, bees humming, the first swallows dipping, long green weeds waving in the water—and the flick and dimple of rising trout putting the tune of adventure into the afternoon?

Or your mind goes back, if you like, to a tussocky, old, rough marsh, the sort of place I was born and bred on, where the landscape marches, dyke-ruled, to the sea-wall. Above it, in the mist of early dawn, the red sails of the oyster smacks glide slowly down the creek, ships sailing above a green and lonely land. Curlew cry and the redshank shriek on the mud. The hoar-frost still hangs heavy on the brown and rattling reeds by the fleet-side. And in on the first breath of dawn, from out of a red and thunderous sky, that rises like the march of armies above the horizon of the sea, come the duck. They swing in from creek and mud-flat, from salting and *zos* grass, from all the lonely places that run on and down a house-less coast.

And you have to be a quick man to get on to them. But when the gun leaps up and the report stabs the half-light of morning, when that splash in the fleet, the sudden mighty plunge of the retriever tells you that you have held straight, then indeed the day is well begun.

Somehow I cannot conceive that the man who sits in a motor-car and considers it sport, the person who chases a golf ball and thinks it hard exercise, the townsman who runs for his train in the morning and sprints for his 'bus in the evening —I cannot believe that these can put quite such heart and courage into the battle of life as the countryman who uses his wits and stretches his muscles in the old arts and the ancient ardours of the chase and the field.

Which is perhaps why we hang on so much longer on the land than they do in towns. There are plenty of men to-day farming the land that their forbears owned or held two and three centuries ago. There are plenty of such men whose fathers and grandfathers knew the slumps and the 'seventies, the riots of the Corn Laws, the upheavals of the Joe Arch period, the burdens thrown upon them by the Franchise Acts.

All these storms have swept over the farmer. They have bowed his head almost to the ground. But, like his own wheat, he has sprung up again when the wind has passed. Like his own hedgerow oaks he has weathered the storms not of a decade, but of a century.

Can the dwellers in town say the same? Usually when once a family takes root in bricks and mortar it is three generations from clogs to clogs.

283

Where are the Whittingtons and the Greshams to-day? Where are the descendants of a hundred families of the great City of London, once mighty as princes in their wealth and possessions? Some have survived. But those whose names have lived on in every case are those whose fathers and grandfathers had sufficient wit and wisdom to put some part of their money in land, to build their houses among green fields, to bring up their children to the simple delights of horses and dogs, guns and rods.

In such things are the faith and future of a race founded. From the sports of the field springs the strength of character which makes the nation mighty, a man confident of himself, able to take knocks with a smile. They are part of the very soul and spirit of the land. Which is why sport will never die so long as a ploughshare turns an English furrow.

SHELD-DUCK

284

III

Hark! Peace!
It was the owl that shriek'd, the fatal bellman
Which gives the stern'st good-night.

WILLIAM SHAKESPEARE
Macbeth

They came over the sea-wall as we were shooting on the marsh, nine of them, sweeping high in wide circles like great inconsequent moths. It was cold, with a bitter touch of frost. And the wind blew easterly, straight from Holland.

The man with me (he was city-bred) said, "What are those great hawks?" They were not hawks at all, but owls, short-eared owls, the Dutch owls of the East Coast, the woodcock owls of Yorkshire. In the North they call them 'woodcock,' for when the woodcock drop in like tired wisps from their long voyage across the North Sea, then also the woodcock owls come drifting in over the sea and sand-dunes, grey and moth-like wraiths in the dusk of autumn afternoons.

These autumn owls possess some sixth sense. Why when there is a plague of voles, shrews, or rats, do these owls, far away on the fens of Holland, the plains of Belgium, the dunes and the marshes of Mecklenburg and Pomerania, suddenly become aware of this new source of food, hundreds of miles away in the island of Britain, across the waters of the North Sea? But they do and they take wing, and on a

285

November afternoon they sweep suddenly in over sea-wall or sand-dune, raiders from a foreign country.

It is as old, as inexplicable, as that urge which sends the lemmings of Norway plunging over the cliffs into the sea in an endless suicidal stream in years when the lemmings themselves threaten to become a plague on the land.

Each year a few short-eared owls breed with us. But you can count them in a county almost on the fingers of each hand. As nesting birds they are rare. But as autumn migrants, in a good year for rats and mice, when a dry summer has bred every rodent that an acre can carry, you will find the short-eared owls flocking into our shores.

They do no harm. On the contrary, they do a great deal of good. No one who sees a short-eared owl soaring in great circles like a buzzard, or beating the marshland levels like a harrier, should shoot it.

I cannot say the same for another foreign owl, that common little beast, that rapacious, cold-blooded murderer, the little owl, *Athene noctua*, the owl of Athene, a bird which carries its screaming victim into a branch and there tortures it slowly, holding its body down with one taloned foot, while with the other it plucks off its head. The little owl will do that again and again to linnets, finches, young partridges, tom-tits, wrens, sparrows.

I have no love for the little owl. See him sitting on a dead branch of a withered tree in full daylight, a small hunched figure in grey feathers with a slit and yellow eye, malevolence personified. Watch that quick, gnat-like flight, quicker than

286

most owls, as he suddenly flickers in long, quick beats from the branch to his quarry, and there binding his victim, tears it slowly to pieces, while the shrieks grow shriller, then fainter.

Lord Lilford turned these foreigners out by the score at Lilford in Northamptonshire about forty years ago. Since then they have spread all over England. To-day in many counties they are the commonest owl of all.

The barn owl, that lovely creature of pure white and soft saffron, is a different matter. He does a world of good. Not long ago I examined the pelts at a barn owl's nest. They consisted of the remains of rats, mice, beetles, voles, and rabbits. Song birds amounted to twenty-three per cent. Game birds were only eight per cent. The rest were ' various.'

So you see that the barn owl does a great deal of good. Watch him beating in the brief light of dusk on slow and silent wings, and you will see him stoop again and again with a sudden noiseless drop, his wings held noiseless above his back, V-shaped above his body. And each time there will be the thin, needle-like squeak of a mouse, or the harder, fighting scream of a rat. But seldom or never the flutter of a partridge, the silly scream of a rabbit.

And I like to have him in my roof-tree, snoring there sonorously like any old parson full of port, screaming sometimes as he stoops above the stable-yard, with an awful blood-curdling hiss that is enough to make any stable-lad's hair stand up straight on end. Half the ghosts of history were barn owls. Half the murdered screams that ring still between the ghostly walls of unroofed baronial mansions and border

287

castles, half the gurgling throttlings of dying knights and maidens trapped by libertines are merely the barn owls digesting their mice.

As for the wood or tawny owls, those excellent creatures with great overarching eyes and terrifying ears, ears that stand up like the horns of satyrs, for these creatures I have the greatest reverence. They are the warders of old woods and stricken oaks, voices of history in glades of bracken.

But these owls are of a homely sort. If you want romance in owls, look for the great eagle owl of Northern France and Germany, a tawny-breasted, tiger-eyed creature, three feet and a half wide, with the clutch of a steel trap. And just occasionally he comes to England. But it is very seldom. I have seen him once, a creature almost as frightening as a tiger seen on foot for the first time.

And there is another owl, the king of the snowline. As big as the eagle owl, but white as the snow, with a breast flecked and spotted. He drifts in sometimes, like a creature of the northern mists, into the bleak and bitter lands of the East Coast, into the chill corries that run inland from Forth and Findhorn, a lost and noble echo.

PINTAIL